D1161547

MANAGEMENT
REDEEMED

Debunking the Fads that
Undermine Corporate Performance

FREDERICK G. HILMER
LEX DONALDSON

THE FREE PRESS

NEW YORK   LONDON   TORONTO   SYDNEY   SINGAPORE

THE FREE PRESS
A Division of Simon & Schuster Inc.
1230 Avenue of the Americas
New York, NY 10020

THE FREE PRESS and colophon are trademarks
of Simon & Schuster Inc.

Manufactured in the United States of America

10   9   8   7   6   5   4   3   2   1

Library of Congress Cataloging-in-Publication Data

Hilmer, Frederick G.
    Management redeemed : debunking the fads that undermine
corporate performance / Frederick G. Hilmer, Lex Donaldson.
        p.   cm.
    Includes bibliographical references and index.
    ISBN 0–684–83162–7
    1. Industrial management.   2. Industrial management—United
States.   3. Comparative management.   I. Donaldson, Lex.   II. Title.
HD31.H492   1996
658—dc20   96–20659
                                                                CIP

To Claire, Sarah, Ben, and Jody Hilmer
and Olwen Donaldson

CONTENTS

INTRODUCTION

"I can tell you in one sentence what most of you are doing wrong today, and how to fix it." At this, the normal undercurrent of shuffling and whispering stopped abruptly. All eyes were on the speaker as the audience of 200 or so executives waited to hear what was coming.

"You don't pay enough attention to your people and customers, and because you've lost sight of these fundamentals, your competitiveness is going to pot . . . it's that simple." The speaker continued: "When you show a visitor around your company, do you let the work force know who is coming and why— or do you take the visitor around, looking at your people working as if they're exhibits in a zoo? When you meet with a customer, do you listen, or do you immediately go into overdrive on how good your company is, and what more you could sell?"

The questions struck a chord. Most of the audience felt at least a bit guilty and hence eager to hear what they needed to do to redeem themselves and improve. What they heard made many of them feel better, and some were even inspired. We, however, were not. We were mad as hell. Why? First, because this lecture was typical of what we see happening to the practice of and writing on management, namely, the substitution of dogma—platitudes, homilies, and fads—for careful, sustained professional management. And second, because otherwise skeptical and pragmatic executives seemed to have put their reasoning powers on hold and were being lulled into believing the messages. The 14-hour days, the years of study, the seemingly endless meetings with customers, colleagues, and subordinates, the agonizing work on budgets and results were all forgotten. Here was an easy way to manage that would solve all their problems! At times, it seems management is incapable of learning from the proverb that the British military historian Liddell Hart used so forcefully in describing what distinguished successful campaigns over many centuries: "In strategy, the longest way round is often the shortest way home."[1]

This book is an attack on the fads and fallacies of modern management and an argument for lifting the practice of management by replacing dogma with the best traditions of the established professions. We believe that those who offer managers success via shortcuts or simplifications are effectively undermining—trivializing and denigrating—the very thing that is in so much need of improvement, namely, the management of large, complex organizations. Other writers have criticized fads in management, but we show how the fads are symptoms of a more fundamental problem—the loss of respect for management and for professional managers.[2] The better way forward, in our view, is to build on what has been learned from both management and other fields of endeavor. It is time for management to be redeemed.

While both of us are mad as hell, it is for quite different reasons. Fred is angry because, as a practitioner of many years and a director of a number of international firms, he sees the quick-fix and fad mentality corrupting the professional practice of management. Today, everyone is a reengineer. Before that they were disciples of flat structures, and before that, of total quality. Along the way they made detours into empowerment, gainsharing, niche marketing, and culture.

Meanwhile, the companies that survive and prosper seem to be doing something else. Firms such as General Electric, Motorola, and Procter & Gamble in the United States and CRA in Australia are consistently pursuing a few simple themes that fit the way they need to be managed in their particular competitive situations. And they stick with these themes for long periods. For Motorola, it has been a 15-year-plus preoccupation with quality. At General Electric, Jack Welch was appointed CEO in 1981, and his "revolution" has been ongoing since then, following a number of consistent themes. For Procter & Gamble, the idea of self-directed teams in relatively flat plant hierarchies has been in place and constantly refined for over 30 years. For CRA, the Australian mining leader, the development of a unique organizational structure and management processes that drive continuous improvement in often remote and diverse locations has been under way since the late 1970s.

These companies all compete in turbulent markets. For them, these are crazy times. But rather than flit from idea to idea or seek a range of crazy solutions, they are dealing with competition and complexity by calmly, purposefully, and professionally developing and adapting sound and seemingly simple ideas. It is excellence in the doing, not the cleverness of their ideas nor nifty jargon, that sets them apart.

Lex is mad as hell about the same thing, but from another viewpoint. Lex is a management scholar who has spent his career researching and writing on organizational design. In Lex's world, good ideas are those that are properly supported by facts and whose logic can withstand the tough criticisms of peers. By these standards, much of what is touted as a pathway to better management is at best unproven and at worst misleading and dangerous. In his most recent research, Lex identified 15 major "new" ways of looking at organizational structure that have been introduced since 1967. A new view of the world every two years! Few, if any, of these ideas stand up to critical analysis, yet each is hailed by its proponents as the "next wave" that will transform management. Lex is mad because novelty seeking seems to be displacing truth seeking in much of the research on management. No wonder that practitioners push a new fad about every two years. Many leading scholars are doing the same thing. If these ideas were well supported and logical one might hail this flow as the beginnings of a vibrant science of management. Unfortunately, this is rarely the case.

Both of us are now professors at the Australian Graduate School of Management, the leading business school in Australia. Our common concern about some trends in modern management, from the viewpoints of both practice and theory, is the basis of this book.

BEWARE OF FADS

The book has two main messages. First, in searching for the elements of good management, we urge managers to beware of fads, of strongly held but largely unfounded beliefs and formulas about how to manage. Rather than offer a pathway to success, prevailing fads have the potential to lead managers down false trails. We discuss five such trails that have been falsified by hype and oversimplification, namely:

- Flatten the structure: Until all hierarchy is abolished, unproductive bureaucracy must be exposed and eliminated.
- The action approach: Don't become immobilized by planning, reflection, or analysis. Allow people to follow their natural instincts and intuition. Focus on visions, not numbers.
- Techniques for all: As problems arise, find the right technique, apply it quickly, and then move on to the next one. There is no situation that can't be fixed by methods such as portfolio planning, value-based planning, niche strategies, total quality management, benchmarking, reengineering, or gainsharing.
- The corporate clan: Model the organization along the lines of a happy family rather than a hierarchy. Create a corporate culture that guides and encourages. Abolish rule books and

procedures manuals and rely on culture to define what is good or bad, right or wrong.

- The directors to direct: Fix the board of directors to better scrutinize management actions and decisions. Make sure that the board chair and a clear majority of directors are tough-minded, independent nonexecutives who are prepared to call the shots and ensure that management keeps the shareholders' interests paramount at all times.

While there are grains of truth in each of these trails, there are also mistaken assumptions and dangerous implications.

MANAGEMENT REDEEMED

Our second message is that there are lessons in the development of established professions such as medicine, law, and engineering that can provide a more useful guide to the practice and teaching of management than the fads and fallacies implicit in the five false trails. We contend that notions of ethics, logic, and action based on learning will be more valuable guides to good management than any quick-fix approach.

Ours is a very positive view of the role of managers in modern society. It undergirds all that we do in working with managers as educators, consultants, and external directors. Instead of applauding quick fixes and standardized methods, we argue for the development of management based on hard, clear thinking. While we see management as parallel to other professions, we recognize that it is still in its infancy. There are thus lessons to be learned by management in the evolution of other professions that sought to develop clear language and to act on the basis of high ethical standards, logic, and proven ideas.

We wrote this book for a number of related reasons. First, we were concerned about the feelings in the community against management. Managers are becoming something of an outcast group in the public mind. The mass media readily portray managers as grossly failing in their duties. The medicine that is prescribed is to reduce the power and authority of managers, curb their status and pay, and, preferably, get rid of large numbers of managers from corporations by downsizing and flattening the hierarchy. We believe such general sentiments to be uncalled for, being based on inaccurate diagnoses of present problems. Moreover, such antimanager moves are potentially very damaging to the competitiveness of our corporations. If management is to be redeemed, a constructive rather than destructive approach is more likely to produce results.

Second, the desire to oversimplify and to reduce complexity is leading to an excessive reliance on simplistic prescriptions as the essential tools of management. In our view, there are no gimmicks that explain sustained success. The best football teams run, pass, block, and tackle with awesome skill based on years of individual and team practice. The best writers spend countless hours crafting and recrafting their manuscripts so that ideas and feelings shine through. Management is no different. The best managers are relentless in the pursuit of facts and reality and in their commitment, energy, and skill in leading groups of people to achieve well-defined and considered goals.

We therefore urge a reassessment of many prevalent management ideas, and call for a renewed appreciation of managers and management. There are few remedies through instant cures; rather, progress comes from the disciplined application of fundamental concepts guided by values and reasoned analysis. Management cannot be successful merely by following general principles or applying generic techniques. Rather, it requires rigorous analysis and the steadfast application of customized approaches and strategies.

We approached this book from our perspective as business school professors, although our backgrounds, in traditional academia and top-level contemporary business practice, are very different.

Fred, a graduate of the Wharton School, spent almost 20 years with McKinsey & Company, Inc., including assignments in

North America, Asia, and Australia, where he headed the firm's Australasian practice. In 1989, he was appointed dean of the Australian Graduate School of Management, and since then has joined the boards of several large international corporations. Fred has written a number of books for practicing managers and recently chaired a Commonwealth committee that produced a major report for the Australian government on competition policy. His experiences made him appalled at the simplistic nature of the prescriptive advice being offered to managers. Much of this "management in three easy steps" literature is too glib to solve the real problems facing corporations. But worse yet, it gives the impression that management is an easy job, thus supporting the popular mood to denigrate managers.

Lex has spent over 20 years researching organizations, including a five-year stint at London Business School and visiting appointments at Stanford and Northwestern. He became convinced that many ideas about managers and business were based on dubious overgeneralizations. Moreover, the prescriptions so freely offered about radical surgery being required for organizations were often wrong. The best analyses from business school research pointed away from the downsize, flatten, and obliterate mentality. Reservations about radical surgery are widely shared among the hard-core research community but have not been widely appreciated by practitioners and the public. Being no stranger to debate and the championing of distinctive viewpoints, Lex resolved to publicly champion his views on these issues. He recently published a book attacking the antimanagement stance of many leading U.S. business school academics. The present book continues this theme in a more practical vein.

This is a book about the management of corporations whose assets and sales are measured in many millions and whose work forces are measured in the thousands and tens of thousands. These organizations play a vital role in local and global business. We contend that these large corporations could be even more valuable and productive if managers better understood the traps in the five false trails, and dedicated themselves to the essence of professional management—or, to put the point another way, were prepared to think beyond the boundaries of management dogma in their pursuit of performance.

We hope that our book will inform our readers who are managers. We trust that it will give them some succor and arm them for the fray. Other readers we hope will be provoked and challenged to reexamine their assumptions. For those given to public commentary about management, we trust that a reading of this book will make them pause before embarking upon their customary litany against managers. For directors of companies, we hope that our book will lead them to a renewed appreciation of their role. Our aim is to enhance all our readers' understanding of the true challenges of management.

1

BEYOND DOGMA

Reengineering is the search for new models of organizing work. Tradition counts for nothing. Reengineering is a new beginning.

—Michael Hammer and James Champy, 1994[1]

We must move beyond change and embrace nothing less than the literal abandonment of the conventions that brought us to this point. Eradicate "change" from your vocabulary. Substitute "abandonment" or "revolution" instead.

—Tom Peters, 1994[2]

If I have seen further it is by standing on the shoulders of giants.

—Sir Isaac Newton, 1676[3]

Which of the above views offers the best guide to successful management in the future? Must everything that has been done and learned up to this point be thrown away? Has nothing useful about good management been discovered from the experiences of the great corporations that have transformed life in this century? Is there no one on whose shoulders those interested in learning about and improving the practice of management can stand? Or is it possible that there is more wisdom in Newton's 300-year-old advice than in contemporary calls for a complete revolution—can true progress come from building on the achievements of the past?

If the debate about management was being judged by what people are saying as opposed to what successful corporations are doing, the answer would be clear. Conventional management is a failure. Radical transformation is the only feasible way forward. Again, to quote from Michael Hammer and James Champy's best-seller, *Reengineering the Corporation*, "the alternative is for corporate America to close its doors and go out of business. The choice is that simple and that stark."[4]

The ideas behind such calls for radical change are often labelled "modern management" or a "new paradigm," and are generally considered a vast improvement over traditional notions of a hierarchically organized firm with defined processes, management structures, and responsibilities. We, however, take the contrary view.

In this chapter, we first outline the ideas behind the calls for transformation and an entirely new approach by categorizing the numerous prevailing fads into five trails that managers are being urged to follow. In the second part of the chapter, we explain why these trails have emerged, why they have found such a ready audience, and what is wrong with them. In the third part we propose an alternative, namely, professional management, an approach that builds systematically and continuously on past achievements in the best traditions of other fields where great advances have been made. The final sections argue that the consequences of following the five false trails blindly and obsessively, rather than encouraging true professionalism in management, is damaging both to firms and to the societies in which they operate.

FIVE TRAILS

The calls for radical transformation and the adoption of a new paradigm reflect a number of commonly proposed fads about modern management: simplify, cut out, cut back, eliminate. Management is being made far too complex and radical surgery is warranted. The titles of the best-selling books tell the story: *Maverick: The Success Story Behind the World's Most Unusual Workplace*,[5] about the iconoclastic South American who transforms traditional manufacturing by letting the employees decide what to do and how; *Made in Japan*,[6] the story of Akio Morita's successful but un-Japanese leadership of Sony; *Zapp! The Lightning of Empowerment*,[7] which describes how quality, productivity, and employee satisfaction are achieved by delegation and empowerment.

These fads can be summarized into five trails as follows:

1. *Flatten the Structure.* Hierarchy is passé, flat is beautiful. Modern companies are like orchestras—one conductor and hundreds of players—not armies with long chains of command. Most organizations are hampered by too many levels of management between the board and the frontline employees who actually invent, make, sell, and provide services. Delayering—downsizing the ranks of middle management in particular—will improve communication, lower costs, speed up decision making, and better motivate all staff to contribute. Less management is better management. And fewer managers are the key.

2. *The Action Approach.* Don't become immobilized by planning and analysis—management is action, not study or reflection: "ready, fire, aim," "do it, fix it, try it," "inspire, empower, lead" rather than "deliberate and administer." Action is always better than the dreaded "paralysis by analysis." Successful managers get their people to move, and movement evolves into strategy as decisions are made in real time. People at the front line have good instincts, opinions of customers are the source of most marketing opportunities, and by stimulating action via empowerment, managers unleash the energy and ideas that are otherwise ignored and stultified by rigorous planning. Put another way, those managers left in the flat organi-

zations of the future shouldn't try to plan, control, or think things through to any great level of detail. Instead, they should set visions, like the oracles of old, and urge the people into action, letting the decisions take shape over time. Intuition, not analysis, is the guiding light. Managers should be like Zen archers, letting the target draw the arrow to it.

3. *Techniques for All.* As problems arise, find the appropriate solution technique and apply it quickly. When the few managers left in place find that vision and intuition are not enough, the good manager need not go back to first principles or hard thinking but instead should pick up and religiously implement the "right" technique or program. This is "instant coffee" management—just open the can and add water—no work required. Modern approaches such as portfolio planning, value-based planning, niche strategies, total quality management, benchmarking, core process reengineering, and gainsharing provide fast and reliable answers to all the tough questions, such as:

   • What business are we really in and how do we compete?
   • How can we get our staff to do things right the first time?
   • How can we dramatically cut costs and waste?
   • How can we provide the sales and service support our customers are demanding?
   • How can we motivate people to innovate and contribute above and beyond the minimum demands of the job?

4. *The Corporate Clan.* Model the organization to be more like a happy family than a hierarchy. Create a corporate culture that guides and encourages. Burn the rule books and procedures manuals. Operate as a clan, in which people understand through shared values what is right and wrong and what is good and bad. Rely on the culture to bring out the best in everyone. East is good, West is bad. They do it this way in Japan, and look at their successes—or so the story goes.

5. *The Board of Directors as Watchdog.* Fix the board to better scrutinize management actions and decisions. Good management flows into the firm from the board of directors. Unless

managers are under the continual scrutiny of a tough-minded board of independent directors, they will fail to perform and, in the worst cases, steal the silver. It is argued that in many countries management has "captured" the board, which then becomes an acquiescent partner in schemes that enrich management or promote its interests ahead of those of shareholders. The remedy: separate the roles of chairman of the board and chief executive and then have the nonexecutive chairman supported by a board with a clear majority of outside part-time directors independent of management influence. The chief executive, and possibly one other executive such as the top financial officer or top operating executive, are the only managers who should be board members, and they ought not serve on committees dealing with board composition, executive remuneration, or auditing. In other words, good management depends on removing management's influence from the boardroom and leaving the direction of the corporation firmly in the hands of part-time outsiders.[8]

The influence of the five false trails on management thought and practice is reflected in language. As Figure 1.1 shows, contemporary management-speak has picked up ingredients of each of the trails. Many of these language shifts are positive, a response to changes in the forces that shape businesses, such as increased global competition and new information, communication, and production technologies. But in other respects, the changing language represents a pendulum that has swung too far toward simplifying and trivializing management, replacing ideas and actions based on sound reasoning with fads and dogma.

THE TROUBLE WITH FADS

What's wrong with these ideas? Aren't they simply putting into words what the best managers and firms are doing? For example, everyone is flattening structures: look at General Electric, Gen-

FIGURE 1.1
THE LANGUAGE SHIFT

	Traditional	New
Structure	Vertical	Horizontal
	Tall	Flat
	Centralized	Decentralized
	Departments	Teams
	Integration	Subcontracting
	Delegate	Empower
Action	Planned	Responsive
	Predictability	Ambiguity
	Analysis	Intuition
	Method	Speed
	Hours	Nanoseconds
Techniques	Mass	Niche
	Efficiency	Quality
	Synergy	Breakup value
	Returns	Options
	Goal setting	Benchmarking
	Remuneration	Gainsharing
Culture	Organization	Clan
	Division	Family
	Standards	Shared values
	Formal	Informal
	Diversity	Homogeneity
	Control	Guide
Board of Directors	Monitor	Strategist
	Passive	Active
	Supporter	Critic
	Rule maker	Police

Source: Much of this chart has been drawn from the pamphlet *Words* by Tom Peters (Palo Alto, California: The Tom Peters Group, 1988).

eral Motors, IBM, ICI. Or look at newer hot firms like Nike, Microsoft, or Benetton, where structures have always been flat. Similarly, the action approach is eloquently expounded by numerous highly regarded managers, from Townsend in *Up the Organization*[9] to Iacocca with his impatience and irreverence for process.[10] "Ready, aim, fire" is for old fuddy-duddies: it is "ready, fire, aim" that characterizes successful modern management.

Techniques, too, are well supported. Quality—think of Motorola or Florida Power & Light. Benchmarking—Xerox and

Procter & Gamble are leading exponents. Value-based planning wins endorsements from senior executives at Pepsico Inc., Merrill Lynch, Lloyds Bank, and Northwest Airlines. Reengineering is blessed by Peter Drucker and put to effective use by Hallmark and Taco Bell. Clans and culture are advocated as an alternative to traditional management on the basis of successes such as McDonald's, Apple, and Nike. And tough action by independent directors is seen as the only way to stop the fish rotting from the head down. Isn't that what saved General Motors, IBM, American Express, and Littlewoods, to name a few cases where boards of directors have replaced CEOs, often after pressure from institutional shareholders?

Practitioners and writers are thus giving these trails the status of present-day conventional wisdom. The case is put so simply, forcefully, and fashionably that any other view sounds untenable, or even politically incorrect. The combined effect, however, is to overthrow much of the sound thinking on good management that has been built up over the years. If followed, the five trails and their underlying fads and prescriptions tear down the sophisticated formal organization and decision systems that corporations have evolved and which make management effective. The problem is that the message is so appealing that it goes down like peaches and cream. The clarity of the message can lull the listener into uncritical acceptance. Since everybody is saying these sorts of things, surely they must be right.

But are they? Can any one or even five ideas explain the past success of firms as diverse as General Electric and McDonald's? And even if the past can be explained, does it follow that what worked in the past will work in the future? Consider, for example, the case of Wal-Mart. Wal-Mart is special. Year after year, sales, profits, and shareholder returns from this massive group of discount stores increase, defying economic cycles and the woes that seem to beset other retailers from time to time. Some argue the reason is market power: Wal-Mart built its business by opening stores mainly in small communities where there was less competition. Once a Wal-Mart store opened in a small town there was no room for another similar retailer. Others point to its systems: electronic linkages with suppliers that keep the shelves well stocked at minimal cost. Another explanation is highly motivated staff, inspired by the late Sam Walton's habit of driving around in a pickup truck visiting stores, and supported by concepts like teamwork and delegation. Paying attention to customers is also mentioned: at Wal-Mart, customers really do come first. And of course leadership, the most intangible but perhaps the most potent factor in management, cannot be ignored.

Which of these is the real cause of Wal-Mart's sustained success? Are all the factors important, are some more important than others, or is there another explanation yet to be discovered?

The honest answer is all of the above. Wal-Mart represents a combination of factors—a thousand infinitesimal actions and decisions—that together have led to its unusual success. A professional seeks to learn from these factors, recognizing that they were developed over more than 25 years and are underpinned by a thoroughness in execution that is the antithesis of fads and quick fixes. Nor does a professional assume that the factors that worked in the past will continue to work in the future.

Why, then, do otherwise hard-nosed and smart managers pick up so willingly on the five false trails and these underlying fads? In a thoughtful review of the emergence and contributions of management "gurus," Andrzej Huczynski, a management academic from the University of Glasgow Business School, concluded that "despite the interest in the timeless procession of business and management fads in the United States and Britain, no convincing explanation of the phenomena has yet been produced."[11] But he notes that management is a fertile field for fads and quick fixes because the problems are intractable, yet the pressure to be seen to be "doing something" is intense. A manager who is using the latest technique supported by an eminent expert or who is following the widely applauded prescriptions of a best-selling book can hardly be criticized, while those who ignore the latest trend risk being judged old-fashioned and unprofessional. Moreover, because many man-

FIGURE 1.2
POSITIVE IDEAS WITHIN FALSE TRAILS

	False Trail	Positive Idea
Structure	Avoid formal structures, hierarchies, and accountabilities: be flexible, ad hoc	Actively use structure, hierarchy, and accountability to direct activities and shape behavior
	Eliminate levels of management relentlessly: flatter is better	Beware of levels of management that add no value
Action	"Just do it"	Keep moving, but be aware of the basis of your actions
	Follow intuition and gut feelings: end "paralysis by analysis"	Respect analysis, data, and reflection as well as intuition
	Keep experimenting, trying new ideas	Distinguish experiments from commitments
Techniques	Techniques provide effective answers	Stay abreast of techniques but be highly skeptical
	One technique suits most situations	Customize the techniques you select
	Keep up with the flow of new techniques	Limit the number of initiatives under way at any one time
Culture	Developing and sustaining culture is management's most critical task	Use clan ideas and culture selectively to reinforce priorities and encourage action
	Ensure that everyone in the organization adopts the same culture	Encourage diversity by including various subcultures in the organization
Board of Directors	Make sure the board keeps management honest and in check	Focus the board on enhancing corporate and top management performance
	Independence of directors is key	Competence and integrity of directors are key

agement problems are complex and persistent, executives often become frustrated. Therefore, the assertion that management is being overcomplicated, that there is a need and way to cut through the web, finds a ready audience.

When examined closely, however, the five trails are shaky or dangerous. They are built on germs of good ideas, as set out in Figure 1.2. But the ideas become false trails when taken too far, as they so often are today. We see the trails as antimanagement. They imply that management is actually simple and requires few managers, preferably under close control by the board. Thus, the false trails contribute to a negative attitude to managers and management in the public mind. This, in turn, fosters an atmosphere ripe for outside intervention in corporate management. While the trails aim to improve the performance of our corporations, they are frequently counterproductive and undermine international business competitiveness.

Why are we mad as hell about this promulgation of the false trails? Because in our view, good management is important to the success of firms and society. Moreover, we contend that there is an alternative to the view of good management embedded in the five false trails.

STAYING ON THE PROFESSIONAL TRACK

If we had to put our alternative into one phrase, it would be "professional management." In using this phrase, our aim is to learn from and build on the positive characteristics of other, more developed professions such as engineering, medicine, veterinary science, law, and architecture. These professions have evolved and continue to exist because society values the impartial and expert application of skill and knowledge. When a profession is seen to depart from core values, its status and legitimacy are immediately attacked, as the current debate about the legal profession illustrates graphically. There is no reason why the field of management could not earn the same respect as other professions.

In our view, a respected profession is distinguished by a number of core values, each of which raises important questions for the practice and teaching of management.

- Professions tend to be based on lofty ideals that transcend self-interest. These ideals might include service to others, creating new knowledge, or, in the case of management,

building and sustaining important, socially productive organizations. For great corporations are important institutions
both nationally and internationally. Their success deter-
mines how well societies are able to improve their lot, and
whether today's investors will be tomorrow's comfortable
retirees. Professionals in pursuit of such a lofty ideal find intrinsic worth and pleasure in their work, and while good
performance brings its rewards, a professional would not
sacrifice the ideal for monetary gain.

- Professionals give form to their ideals by mastering a craft or
  body of knowledge. Such mastery takes years of learning
  and experience. There is rarely, if ever, a single best way to
  acquire the knowledge. College and graduate education as
  well as the school of hard knocks are important.

- A professional body of knowledge is based on sound reasoning, not dogma or unproven rules. However, professionals
  recognize that there are different kinds of reasoning, all of
  which have a role to play. Sometimes reasoning is based on
  the analysis of data, sometimes it entails critical analysis of
  precedents and cases, and sometimes it reflects aesthetic
  and qualitative factors, as in product design or architecture.
  Professionals do not shy away from understanding the basis
  of the knowledge they seek to apply, and are willing and able
  to criticize current beliefs.

- Reasoning, especially in fields such as management, rests on
  the ability to use language clearly and precisely. In management, people often use the same words but mean quite different things because they have different understandings
  and education. For example, a manager agreeing to "participation" with a work group may mean quick consultation before a decision is made by him. The work group, however,
  may think it has been given a veto right over any action, or
  that only it can decide what is to be done. Without clear language, effective communication and sound decision making
  become impossible, the body of knowledge about effective
  management cannot be advanced, and dogma prevails.

- Professions operate according to high ethical and technical standards. They respect both the letter and the spirit of the laws that govern their operations. And they expect that all members of the profession acquire and apply their knowledge and skill carefully and diligently.

Members of a profession thus tend to be highly skilled, independent, and able to balance loyalty to the ideals of their calling with the demands of those who hire them. The blindly obedient "corporation man" could not be a professional. Nor could the person who flits from one quick fix to another, or unquestionably accepts dogma.

How would a professional deal with the fads reflected in the five false trails? Clearly, a professional would not simply cast the five trails aside. Instead, he or she would seek out the ideas of value, skillfully navigating some of the more pronounced fads and fallacies of modern management and choosing elements that fit the needs and situation of the specific firm at a specific time. In our view, a professional would draw from each trail the positive ideas set out in Figure 1.2, but would apply even these ideas carefully and selectively.

THE IMPACT ON FIRMS

Not taking the professional approach and blindly following the five false trails is costly both to firms and to society as a whole. The performance of firms is undermined in two ways.

First, the five false trails can encourage managers to do the wrong things for their specific situation—to train for swimming when the race is to be held on land. For every case where each of the five trails may be true there is another where each is wrong. For example, flat structures are no guarantee of high performance, and may put some parts of a business at risk. Who would feel confident flying in an airliner if the different maintenance crews handling the planes acted independently of each other or if, instead of centralized air traffic control, the people flying the airplane acted autonomously from the work group in the control tower? Planning—as opposed to acting—can be easily ridiculed as "overintellectualizing" by those who find any form of rigorous thinking objectionable, but how else can the complex set of activities needed to deliver modern products and services in many large firms be coordinated? Techniques are no better than their application—that is why most reengineering or quality initiatives fail. Similarly, equating the management of a business with the culture of family life or tribal rituals can often be simplistic or worse, in that it denies the internal diversity that is an asset for the modern corporation. And finally, one-line prescriptions for how to structure boards of directors have been around for decades, yet there is reason to believe that they are irrelevant or that acting on them might harm rather than help. Creating a winning corporation isn't as easy as appointing a board of nonexecutive directors.

Second, even when the trail heads in the right direction, its prescriptions implicitly encourage poor implementation. Why? Because managers who believe the potions will work instantly fail to persevere when results don't appear quickly. Also, because these managers think the trail is easy, they take on too many initiatives—an overdose of instant remedies. Overly optimistic time frames and work overload follow from damaging platitudes such as "flatten structure" or "action counts." Hence, most of the false trails either don't go anywhere or hold up progress.

Jack Welch's story at General Electric illustrates the point.[12] It took over four years for Welch's efforts to begin to bear fruit in terms of productivity, despite a spate of activity and many hard decisions in his early years as CEO. When Welch was appointed in 1981, productivity across GE was increasing at about one percent to two percent per annum. Welch set a six percent per annum goal for improving productivity, and by all accounts drove the organization relentlessly to achieve it. However, in 1986, productivity growth still hovered around two percent. The big jump did not occur until 1987—six years after Welch's

appointment—when five percent was achieved. The six percent target was finally met in 1989.

Most managers, however, after two years of effort without
dazzling results, tend to lose confidence in the idea they began
with, and start looking for another solution. Nor are investors
and fund managers, at least in the West, likely to remain patient
for long periods. The experience of the Japanese and the Americans with total quality management shows this. In the 1960s,
the Japanese were working on quality, while the Americans
were into management by objectives. In the 1970s, the Americans adopted T-Groups and participation, while the Japanese
continued to strive for quality. In the 1980s, the Americans
shifted to strategic planning, mergers, and restructuring.
Meanwhile, the Japanese stuck with managing quality. Eventually, the Americans discovered "total quality management" and
wondered why the Japanese were so far ahead in managing for
quality. The good news is that, after ten or more years of
change in major firms, many U.S. companies are catching up,
and some, like Motorola, are forging ahead.

THE COST TO SOCIETY

The five false trails don't just mislead individual managers and
firms. They also have a more widespread cost to the societies
that allow these ideas to flourish. When the five false trails
combine with heightened public interest in management and
economics, a self-reinforcing cycle of costly misunderstanding
and frustration begins. The result is to limit business and job
opportunities for domestic firms, and to surrender areas of
growth to overseas firms based in societies that are not trapped
in this cycle.

The cycle portrayed in Figure 1.3 is triggered by the top two
factors, first the misunderstanding of the essentials of management (encouraged by the widespread promulgation of the five
false trails) and second, the heightened public interest in and
awareness of management and economics. No longer is man-

FIGURE 1.3
A COSTLY CYCLE

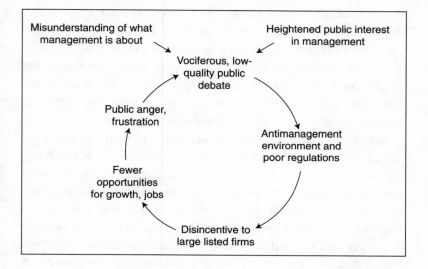

agement an arcane, back-page topic. Business now vies with sports in terms of media coverage. Stories about megastar managers—Bill Gates, Michael Eisner—rival coverage of sports stars such as Steffi Graf or Greg Norman. Business mistakes—bankruptcies, losses in financial markets—are given more attention than the failure of a sports team to make the play-offs.

People are more interested in business and management because they cannot help being involved. Effective management is central to a society's success. And almost everyone's savings are tied up in funds that invest in "securities," paper that is only as secure as the competence of the managers in the firms that issue it and the professionals who manage the money. Moreover, the amounts of money involved are big—large corporations inevitably make decisions involving billions and crossing state and national boundaries. In many respects, regional and national politics has been overridden by global business.

The combination of heightened public interest and public misunderstanding is, however, dangerous. What follows is a vociferous, low-quality public debate colored by the politics and rhetoric of blame and quick fixes. The Monday-morning quarterbacks from the media and politics always know what to do, especially after the event: "Sack the board" ... "Top management must go" ... "Better management is needed" ... "Listen to the customer" ... "Cut executive pay." These familiar catchcries then trigger the next step in the cycle: an unattractive antimanagement environment and poor regulation of large, management-intensive businesses.

Yet these simplistic answers are almost always ill-suited to the complexities of business. Modern societies rely on three types of organizations. First are businesses run by owners who put up their own money and sweat equity. These are typically quite small, though with some visible exceptions. Second are large publicly listed companies, where the risk capital needed is usually well beyond the reach of any one individual or tightly knit group. Risk capital is generally provided via the listing and trading of shares on a stock exchange. These firms are critical to modern economies, covering most high-technology and large-scale manufacturing and service sectors. The third type of organization is the government owned-and-operated entity or highly regulated firm, usually providing services in areas where markets are believed to be unable to deliver what the public wants. Examples range from police, prisons, and education to utilities or "natural monopolies" such as public transport and electricity grids.

While this description of the three types of organizations is broad brush, the key point is that modern societies need a variety of organizational forms. Big firms don't run small businesses well, smothering them with red tape, while small businesses can't develop the next jet engine or communications network. When societies cut out or hamstring one of these types of organization (e.g., the private firm in the old communist world), they suffer. Put another way, the ability of a society to encourage and support different types of organizations to do different tasks is critical if it is to develop economically and socially.

An Antimanagement Bias

However, when there is poor public understanding of and debate about the role of management, what follows is typically an unattractive environment for, and then excessive regulation of, at least one type of organization: large, publicly listed, management-intensive firms such as General Motors, General Electric, IBM, Kodak, Disney, ICI, Toyota, Sony, Siemens, and Samsung.

If one had to choose a single word to describe this environment, it would be "antimanagement." Put most bluntly, the false trails are saying that there are too many managers and that even those few who are needed overcomplicate their work and, when given the chance, put their own interests ahead of the organization's.

The antimanagement bias is revealed in surveys showing that, in Western societies, people trust their doctors, pharmacists, and teachers, but rank managers and salespeople toward the bottom with politicians. Managers are seen to have made jobs for themselves and then to have captured the benefits by raising money from an unsuspecting public, treating work forces badly, acting shortsightedly, and overpaying themselves. It is thus not surprising that there is wide support for calls to regulate the raising of capital, to force more disclosure of what managers are doing, to regulate pay, training, and working conditions, and to hold directors liable for everything that might go wrong in a company. Figure 1.4 illustrates this point. In almost every Western society there is one trend that seems unstoppable—the inexorable rise in detailed regulation of business, especially of larger publicly owned firms.

For example, raising capital by issuing a prospectus has become a legal minefield. And laws with respect to safety and employment practices often assume that managers don't care about the welfare or development of employees rather than assuming that high safety standards and fair employment practices are in everyone's interest.

Interference in the management of large corporations

FIGURE 1.4

CONSEQUENCES OF AN ANTIMANAGEMENT ENVIRONMENT

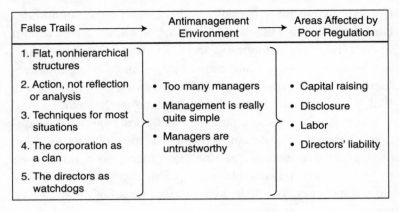

abounds today, not only by government regulation but in other ways. The hysteria in the business press against managers has led to cases of investor and board confidence in CEOs being eroded before hard-fought turnaround plans have had a chance to produce the goods. For example, only two years after the American Express board removed James Robinson, replacing him with Harvey Golub, *Fortune,* in a lead article on the company, began by questioning "whether Harvey Golub . . . is up to the job."[13] The fact that in two years the share price had risen from $25 to $44 was dismissed as due mostly to "cost cutting." That repositioning and reviving a brand in a competitive global market might take at least five years or even longer was not seriously considered. This kind of attitude undermines managerial authority and replaces planning by quick fixes.

The fashionable doctrine of investor activism for the institutions has led to officials from insurance companies or pension funds meeting with CEOs and expecting them to divulge details of their strategies. If the CEO declines to answer invasive questions then he or she will be pilloried as closed-minded and secretive. Yet if the CEO does divulge secrets in confidence to these big investors, the CEO will be accused of facilitating insider trading and discriminating against small shareholders. The answer will be more calls for regulation by government to stop insider trading! Thus, intervention breeds more intervention. The intent is to boost organizational effectiveness, but the upshot may be quite different.

THE CONSEQUENCES

Where does all this lead? Some experts see the eventual decline of the public firm. Corporations are eager to go private, explore any form of financing other than public equity, take on debt, or arrange management or investor buyouts to escape from regulatory burdens and scrutiny. For those small firms that are becoming bigger, these trends lead entrepreneurs (a sadly tinged word) to think again before involving public shareholders in the business. The cost of being big, public, and visible are seen as too high. The point was vividly made by an entrepreneur owner of a billion-dollar-plus international company whose expansion and development would have been accelerated by a public capital raising: "I couldn't tolerate the interference—it would kill the vitality of my business."

Societies that bias the environment against the large publicly managed firm pay a price in lost opportunities. There are many existing and emerging fields in which only large public companies can compete. Automobiles, steel, high-technology manufacturing, computing, telecommunications, resources, utilities, and service chains have reached a size and complexity that prevent all but the largest firms from succeeding. Societies, especially the Japanese and the "Asian tigers" that are hospitable to large management-intensive firms, have done particularly well in these fields. Conversely, the West has seen much of its industrial base become "rust belts" as opportunities have shifted offshore.

The opportunities that are lost are not simply the result of a lack of inventiveness. It was British Leyland that conceived the Mini-Minor car, but it was Toyota that dominated the world's small-car market. The color copier was invented in Adelaide, Australia, but the economic benefit was gained in Japan. Koreans didn't invent microwave cookers, but Samsung has built a global business in the field. Societies that undermine their large public firms should not be surprised when they lose out in areas where these types of firms are vital.

The cycle doesn't stop here. As opportunities are lost, public anger and frustration with management grow, fueled by continuing faulty understanding. So shouting headlines appear: "Jobs going offshore" . . . "Japanese managers are kicking our butts" . . . "Management education is leading our firms astray" . . . "The MBA is obsolete" . . . "New management paradigms urgently needed." The mistaken belief set underpinned by the five false trails is reinforced: more regulation, scrutiny, condemnation is the order of the day. And so the cycle goes on.

There is another secondary effect of this public misunderstanding of management and the vital role of large firms. This is an erosion of confidence in the future. If management is widely seen as corrupt and inept, if large firms are believed to be obsolete, if everything is to be radically changed because nothing is working, what will consumers and employers do? Take fewer risks, save more, spend less, and prepare for the decline of a major source of employment in society. These beliefs can become a dangerous self-fulfilling prophecy. If we believe the future will be bad we invest less and take fewer risks on new ideas or new products: fewer opportunities are then created and the bleak outlook becomes reality.

Misunderstanding is always costly. Misunderstanding in a field that has become central to modern societies—namely management—is particularly costly, and it will become more so. A first step in gaining a better understanding is to see through fads and misleading ideas—this is the aim of the next five chapters. A second is to develop an alternative, better way to think about, practice, and teach management, a subject covered in the final two chapters.

2

FLATTEN THE STRUCTURE

"Our organization is paralyzed by the smiling dead hand of middle management," complained the general manager. "Whenever I want to take an initiative, do something different, rock the boat, I see the smiles and nods of agreement . . . but nothing happens. Things just seem to go on in the same old ways. If I kick and scream I get fewer smiles and more nods but still no sustained action . . . what do I do?" The guru's answer: "Flatten the structure. You suffer from too many levels of management. Ideally you, the boss, should be able to communicate your initiatives directly to the front line, the people who actually make things happen. Every level between you and them distorts and slows your message. Your company will do more with fewer layers, fewer middle managers."

The guru, like all good gurus, has pointed to a fad the manager might follow. But he has also left many unanswered questions. How flat should the organization be? One level, three, seven? What should the people at each level be doing to make the company work better, communicate faster? How do the large numbers of people at each level coordinate activities and maintain uniform standards? The gurus are silent on these issues. However, they seem certain that, whatever the number of levels in the structure today, removing some will be an improvement. Practitioners have heeded the call. As Gerry Mitchell, former president of the U.S. industrial firm Dana Manufacturing, who organized his 15,000-strong work force into five levels of management, said, "Five is better than six, and when we can get to four, we will do it."[1] Or as a senior IBM manager observed as the company struggled with yet another reorganization, "We have taken out some levels, but this is just the beginning . . . We may not need managers at all—only people who deal with customers and products."

The belief that flatter is better is a strong one. The idea that middle management is inherently destructive, or at least unnecessary, has enormous popular appeal. Books, articles, seminars uncritically repeat the claim, as story after story is told of how productivity, quality, morale, communication, and even profits improved after the knife was put through middle management. The flatten-the-structure theme is reflected in a number of fads including delayering, downsizing, rightsizing, inverting the pyramid, and replacing managers with communication and computing technologies. Yet the flatter-is-better school is a false trail, one that, followed avidly, undermines performance by offering limited benefits while exposing the company to high risks. Large organizations exist because they can provide services by coordinating the actions of thousands of people. Hierarchy is one powerful way this is done, though not an easy organizational structure to make work. But throwing hierarchy and structure away is hardly a sensible response, especially when alternative methods of direction and coordination have yet to be developed.

In this chapter we critically examine and disprove the notion that flatter is better, arguing that there will be a continuing need for hierarchy and structure. Moreover, we assert that, properly used, hierarchy and structure can help managers achieve and sustain high levels of organizational performance. We first rebut the most popular arguments against hierarchies. Contrary to widespread and popular assertions, hierarchies do not necessarily lead to bloated costs, poor communications, and low levels of customer service. Moreover, data processing and communication technologies are enhancing, not replacing, the essential work of managers and thus support rather than supplant the idea of hierarchy. Second, drawing on both corporate examples and academic research, we recap the main arguments in favour of hierarchy, showing why it is an effective way to manage large, complex organizations. Third, we take an example, Dana Manufacturing, to illustrate the limited benefits and significant risks of blindly pursuing the flatter-is-better trail.

We conclude the chapter by outlining what we see as the real issue with structure—how to design and put in place a hierarchy that works by effectively allowing modern, educated work forces to use their talents and efforts rather than simply abolishing what seems ugly or hard. The key, in our view, is not to become obsessed with flatter is better, but rather to actively use structure and hierarchy to direct activities and shape behavior so that the corporation is successful in both the short and longer term.

FOUR MYTHS

Most management organizations are set up as hierarchies. People at the front line report to a manager. These managers, in turn, are responsible to other managers in a chain that extends to the top of the company. The chains are usually drawn as a pyramid, some being steep and tall (bad) and others being flat (good). In many large organizations, there can be ten or more levels of management—foreman, supervisor, facility manager, district manager, area manager, country manager, business unit manager, sector manager, group manager, and finally chief executive, not to mention assistants, deputies, advisers, and support staff. This formidable array is typically designed to coordinate and direct the activities of the thousands of people who create, make, sell, and provide services to customers.

Despite decades of consulting expertise and the extensive experience of large firms in designing and redesigning structures, these hierarchies are invariably frustrating.

This is particularly the case when a hierarchy becomes taller than necessary for carrying out its functions. Yet, because the rationale for hierarchy is often poorly understood, managers unwittingly make the hierarchy taller to deal with problems that could better be dealt with in other ways. For example, a manager struggling to cope with both technical and operational matters often finds it easier to add a level of organization, such as "assistant vice-president, technical" or "assistant vice-president, field services," rather than look more fundamentally at the way the structure operates and the competence of the people. Levels are added like Band-Aids to the point where they no longer function well. The hierarchy becomes taller than necessary, cumbersome, indecisive, and ineffective. The response is then the draconian one—get rid of hierarchy completely by radical flattening rather than by facing the real problems, such as the appropriateness of processes, product/service mix, cost structures, or staff, and then redesigning the hierarchy itself.

No matter how many examples of effective hierarchies surround us, many consultants, executives, and members of the business press continue to attack the idea of a hierarchical, multilevel structure. Four myths are put forward. Hierarchies are not necessary, they first argue; organizations should operate like an orchestra, with each person independently playing his role. Second, they say hierarchies inflate overheads, leading to excessive costs that can be avoided in a flat structure. Third, hierarchy is accused of killing communication between management, customers, and frontline employees, thus leading to poor service and low-quality goods. The answer: invert the hierarchy and make the customer king. Finally, critics contend that hierarchy will become quite unnecessary as new computing and communication technologies take over the decision-making and information-transfer roles of most managers. Close scrutiny of successful organizations and proven theory high-light the fallacy of each of these claims.

The Orchestra Myth

One argument against hierarchy in modern corporations, graphically put forward by Peter Drucker, paints the modern organization as an orchestra in which a single conductor pro-vides guidance to a hundred or more players, each of whom is a highly skilled expert.[2] If the work force were similarly expert, why not use the orchestra model? Each worker is trained in a part, and the parts are designed to mesh perfectly. Where inno-vation is needed, the model switches to the improvisation seen in jazz bands.

What the orchestra model is saying is that the solution to the problems of poor communication, bloated costs, and excessive red tape is to get rid of hierarchy. The good organization is the flat or flattened organization. Managerial positions and man-agers are to be removed. Salaries and perks for managers are to be cut. Any reference to managers planning rather than doing is denigrated as bureaucratic nonsense and not real work. Communications, rather than being restricted to flow through the levels of the hierarchy, are to be free-flowing and multichannel so that anyone speaks to everyone else.

The appealing idea of the company as an orchestra evapo-rates with even a little scrutiny. In a business, where is the score with each note defined in terms of tone, loudness, and tempo? The orchestra functions only when everyone plays his defined part exactly as written by the composer. And where, in a business, is the composer? Who is brilliant enough to write the score for General Electric or Sony or Mercedes Benz? What would it look like? Even if we soften Drucker's analogy and say business is like a jazz band in which expert players know each other well and can improvise, the analogy still fails. In a jazz band, too, there is clear discipline and hierarchy. You never see everyone improvising at once, the trombones for example, each going their own way. Moreover, jazz bands that improvise are usually quite small; larger ones only allow certain players, such as the lead trumpeter, to improvise.

The orchestra model relies on the CEO's ability to directly supervise and talk to all employees, something now believed possible with modern video technology. However, research on communication does not support the idea that direct communication with the work force is preferable to communication via the hierarchy. Not surprisingly, research on effective communication in organizations shows the following:[3]

- Packaged CEO messages usually fail. The CEO's corporate video or "sermon from the mount" is rarely effective with the front line. Leaving aside language issues (most large firms don't have a work force uniformly fluent in the CEO's language), CEOs operate, and should operate, at a level of abstraction that is too general for most frontline staff. "Dynamic" . . . "results-oriented" . . . "competitive" . . . "customer-driven" . . . "caring" are terms that are quite meaningful to senior managers and that, for example, drive their redesign of performance evaluation and pay systems, budgets, and market research initiatives. But what is the truck driver or clerk or programmer or salesperson supposed to do differently? Unless these ideas are thought through and made much more specific, the only message that is heard by the work force is the frustrating "try harder and do better."
- People listen most carefully to their direct supervisor. Communication from a direct supervisor in terms that show how the work of individuals will be affected is given most credibility by the work force. People listen when there is an element of "what's in it for me" in the message. Moreover, people tend to trust messages from supervisors they know more than communications from the corner office.
- One-way communication doesn't work. For example, communication from employees dries up if they feel they aren't being listened to, a conclusion they quickly reach when little happens after suggestions are made. Who is best able to deal

with suggestions and keep the workers involved in the picture? Not the CEO. The direct supervisor, on the other hand, in a well-designed organization, is ideally placed to listen and then make things happen either in the area being supervised or by working with colleagues or senior managers.

Research in communication thus demonstrates that hierarchies should not be collapsed but rather set up to allow people in organizations to effectively talk and listen. Thus, the orchestra model of the organization—one CEO directly communicating with all employees—is beguiling but false.

It is ironic that making a structure too flat or too tall produces similar problems. In a too-tall structure, the numerous levels frustrate communications between the CEO and the front line. Similarly, when the structure is too flat, the overloaded supervisor cannot cope with all the communications and decisions. Reports from subordinates languish on the desk. News from upper management cannot get through the supervisor to subordinates, because the supervisor is too busy with other things. Communications both up and down the hierarchy are choked in a bottleneck. Thus, a too-flat structure is as much a barrier to communication and decision making as is a too-tall structure.

A diluted form of the orchestra model is "managing by walking around" (MBWA). The CEO is urged to manage by personally visiting the shop floor and frontline office, talking directly with lower-level employees. Shoe leather is to replace paper. In this way, the manager learns directly what is happening "on the firing line" and can resolve issues on the spot by exercising authority face-to-face with the workers. The CEO is no longer remote, hiding on the top floor in a plush office. The organization is thus acting like an orchestra even if middle managers remain. The problems with this approach are well put in the following witty definition:

> **Management by walking around** *n*. The practice of a CEO who, while expanding his ambit of mischief, proves he could not possibly have come up through the ranks.[4]

While MBWA does have a positive side, the technique must be used sparingly because it subverts hierarchy and thus becomes counterproductive. Who is the worker or salesman to believe—the CEO, seen rarely but with unquestioned power, or the direct supervisor? If the worker or salesman believes the CEO, where does this leave the direct supervisor? The supervisor will feel that his authority has been undermined and that he is not really part of the management team. What MBWA is best understood as saying is that there is value in senior management's visiting and being seen at the front line. But to imply that the occasional walking tour is a substitute for management, that it is anything like a conductor's leadership of an orchestra, is nonsense.

The Myth of Bloated Overheads

A second argument against hierarchies is that they inflate costs. Contrary to popular belief, hierarchies, rather than leading to bloated overheads, are actually more efficient than large organizations of loosely linked autonomous units that are in essence like a family of small firms. The myth of the cancerous growth of administrators as the inevitable consequence of hierarchy was made famous as Parkinson's Law.[5] Parkinson's humorous, satirical book develops a "law" based on descriptions of hypothetical, giant, often civil service, bureaucracies. According to this law, managers will strive to increase the number of subordinates in order to boost their own status, power, and salary, even if there is no real work for those subordinates to do. Parkinson's Law describes a sort of cancer whereby managers breed more of their ilk, burdening the organization with unproductive overheads that stifle real work. *Parkinson's Law and Other Studies in Administration* is widely read and frequently used in seminars and after-dinner speeches on the topic of management, despite its being merely a satire. Its humor adds to its appeal. It seems to say pithily what many people believe to be all too true.

If Parkinson's Law were true, the percentage of employees who were managers would rise as the organization grew. However, studies of actual organizations fail to find this swelling of managerial ranks. A series of studies by Professor Peter Blau, then at the University of Chicago,[6] found no evidence that the percentage of managerial and administrative personnel rose as organizational size grew. In fact, he found that the percentage declined. This led him to state that organizations show an economy of scale in administration. Subsequent work continues to validate Blau's findings.[7]

For many people, it is self-evident that organizations become top-heavy with managers as they grow, because the hierarchy becomes taller. There are therefore more levels and managers relative to workers. While Blau found elements of this true, he also discovered offsetting processes not apparent to the casual observer. Larger organizations have more experience in the type of work done by each person and work group than small organizations because they typically handle large volumes of similar work. With this experience supervision becomes easier: the span of control at each level in the hierarchy becomes greater as organizational size increases. Thus, in a larger organization, any one supervisor is looking after more workers and any one manager is looking after more supervisors and so on up the hierarchy. Larger organizations also use more standard procedures and this economizes on managerial time, further facilitating broader spans of control. For example, a computerized payroll installed when there are 50 employees can also cope with 500 employees with little further managerial attention required. The result of these processes is that the taller hierarchies in larger organizations actually oversee a relatively larger base of workers. Put simply, the ratio of 'chiefs to Indians' actually declines as organizations grow larger.

With greater organizational size, administrative work becomes proceduralized and specialized, and much of it can be delegated to administrative and support staff. However, the administrative and support staff decreases as a percentage of total employees as organizations grow, so again, overhead costs are kept down. Larger organizations can afford more investment in systems and processes that improve managerial productivity. Take, for example, the case of General Mills Restaurant Group (GMR), described by Professor James Brian Quinn of Dartmouth in his award-winning book, *Intelligent Enterprise*.[8] GMR operates chains of restaurants including Red Lobster, Olive Garden, and Bennigan's. It has been growing at 15 percent or more per annum. But, through improved information and control systems, as it has grown, the number of restaurants reporting to a single supervisor has doubled, so the number of managers has not had to be increased in line with the growth in the organization. The economies of administration were highlighted when GMR acquired a chain of 27 restaurants and found that the systems and processes in the smaller chain required as many managers as GMR's 400 other restaurants. The point is not that hierarchy should be or can be obliterated. Rather, it is that as firms grow, hierarchies can be and generally are made more efficient.

There have been many research studies of the percentage of managerial and administrative personnel among total employees.[9] These have been conducted on many different types of organizations across many industries and countries. Almost all studies fail to find cancerous growth. Most find either scale economies, as Blau did, or a neutral position of managerial administrative personnel growth in proportion with production workers. Thus, the best academic research and objective evidence disagree sharply with the doom and gloom of Parkinson and the raucous chorus of organizational gurus. Moreover, they have done so for many years. Yet commentaries continue to abound that rely on instinct and the hoary old fables of Parkinson. Such commentaries misinform policy. They lead to prescriptions that organizational growth must be interrupted to root out the excessive managerial overhead. They lead to prescriptions of massive surgery to rip out the cancer, when in fact there is no disease.

The Myth of the Inverted Hierarchy

A third myth about hierarchy is that it kills communication between management, customers, and frontline employees. As a result, service and quality are said to suffer. The antidote is not only to abolish but also to invert the hierarchy, as Jan Carlzon reportedly did while running the Scandinavian airline SAS.[10]

According to popular wisdom, an upright (as opposed to inverted) hierarchy distorts communication. The longer the chain of command, the more opportunities there are for distortion. If people at the top of organizations can't hear what their customers and staff are saying, they quickly lose touch and make poor decisions. The people at SAS didn't provide indifferent service because they disliked their customers—they simply weren't hearing the dissatisfaction or seeing the opportunities to do something the customer would prefer. In that case, not just flattening the structure but also turning it upside down, with the customer on top, was seen as critical to improving service.[11]

The result is that at seminars today, a popular notion is the inverted hierarchy, as adopted by SAS. In this party piece, the presenting CEO takes an organizational chart and turns it upside down, so that he is at the bottom and the workers and customers are at the top. This act of sacrilege is sure to shock or get a cheer. It dramatizes the points that the CEO should be accessible to customers and the workers should be treated with dignity. However, we note that at the end of the talk the CEO is still the CEO.

Inversion of hierarchy is a valuable concept only if used sparingly and carefully. Used indiscriminately it is counterproductive. When the CEO holds the organizational chart upside down he is sending a symbolic message that everyone in the organization is serving the customer, because even the CEO is serving the customer. Spending time on the shop floor with the production workers or at the counter tending to customers has some positive benefits. The CEO gets to appreciate the trials and tribulations of the front line firsthand. The CEO takes the pulse of workers and customers directly. Senior management is seen as more accessible and caring than it might otherwise be seen. But most CEOs and senior managers probably only spend about one day per month acting in this role. To claim that this is inverting the hierarchy is, at best, heady rhetoric. The rest of the time, the CEO is acting as the CEO.

Similarly, the CEO may have a policy of being available to deal with customers directly. But in practice, this may be half an hour a day so that, again, most time is spent on executive managerial duties. The CEO may spend significant chunks of time dealing directly with major customers who are crucial to the well-being of the company—sometimes on a CEO-to-CEO basis. However, this kind of key client work relationship is part of normal top management duties, so it is not a radical break with hierarchy, nor is it necessarily new.

Thus, while managerial behaviors claimed to be an inversion of the hierarchy may be valuable, they are not really an inversion of the hierarchy. In fact, the point is that the top manager goes down to meet the workers and customers but remains the top manager—the CEO does not become a worker. Without the CEO's retaining the power and status of the office there would be little point to the exercise, since the CEO could not fix problems the workers were powerless to fix and the morale boost of rubbing shoulders with the CEO would be lost. The key to such practices is that the person who comes down to the shop floor is the person from the top of the hierarchy. This is not an inversion of the hierarchy but a way to reinforce the hierarchy by making it work more effectively.

The wise CEO spends most time in the top manager role. There are many matters that rise to the top of the pyramid for the attention of the CEO because he or she alone possesses the authority, perspective, and experience to deal with them. The delegation of authority down the hierarchy, though valuable, is always limited by the way delegations are defined. It is impossible to anticipate every eventuality when specifying the authority of subordinates. And delegation is always constrained by the requirement to contain risks such as those involved in large expenditures or ventures into new areas. The CEO has to be at his or her job handling those issues. If the CEO spends excessive time on the shop floor, too many big issues go begging and the organization as a whole ceases to operate effectively. Only the CEO can handle critical policy and integrative decisions, whereas shop floor work and customer service can be done by frontline personnel quite adequately.

The point is demonstrated vividly by the experience in Australia of Budget Rent-A-Car. The Budget franchise was originally owned by Bob Ansett, a charismatic and service-oriented manager who excelled in motivating staff, being out in the branches, serving customers personally on a regular basis, and leading by example via an inverted hierarchy. But under Ansett's leadership Budget failed. One likely reason: inadequate top management attention to financing, pricing, and strategy. A more conventional hierarchy might well have ensured that these critical matters were not ignored.

The Technology Myth

A fourth myth cited in favor of abolishing hierarchy is that technology, especially computing and communications, will replace most of the work done by "middle management." According to this argument, technology will replace much of the calculation and analysis on which decision making is based. More importantly, instantaneous communication—e-mail, video conferencing, voice mail, interactive databases—will allow direct communication among all parts of an organization, customers, and suppliers without management filtering and summarizing. These arguments, however, miss the point that real managers are neither calculating machines nor nodes in electronic networks that automatically summarize, reroute, and highlight information. Computers are good at taking numbers and running calculations. In this way, they continue to take over the jobs of employees doing routine calculations. Hence, in insurance companies the army of clerks who processed renewals and claims, sitting in large halls in rows of desks, has been replaced by computers with a few operatives to enter the data received from clients. Clearly, there is much potential to further computerize processing of numbers. In the future, electronic links will increasingly connect the firm, its suppliers, and customers, for example, by home shopping.

But it is untrue that this trend of computerization will be extended much up the hierarchy to middle managers. Their work can be computerized only if it, too, consists of processing data according to rules. Yet most work performed by middle managers does not consist of simply applying rules. Little of their day is spent performing calculations. While the manager may look at some numbers such as sales orders, service levels, or costs, he or she typically has to combine them with more qualitative information, such as estimates as to when a back order will be filled or when a new machine will be operating properly. These qualitative aspects are a mixture of facts and perceptions; often they involve little more than guesses based upon past experience that the manager possesses. And nearly always the mix of hard, quantitative data and soft, qualitative "guesstimates" has to be combined through a process that involves judgment. Newer approaches such as "expert systems," used for deciding routine loans from banks, replace human judgment, but these are only useable on the more routine decisions that are not part of the real managerial work in these organizations.

With the advent today of electronic mail, the Internet, and the Worldwide Web, people are very aware of a second major use of technology: for communication. Computers have a great capacity to move numerical data, words, and graphics very rapidly between different people and different places. This, in turn, leads to the idea that middle managers will become redundant because their job of passing information from the bottom of the hierarchy to the top, that is, from the firing line to the strategic apex and vice versa, will be taken over by computers. Since computers work faster and more accurately than humans, computerization will improve this task, we are told, and so the elimination of tiers of middle managers will actually improve information flow, making the demise of middle managers certain. After all, aren't middle managers just noisy conduits or unnecessary filters between bottom and top?

We answer: 'No!' Middle managers are not just passing on information. They summarize, edit, interpret, synthesize, resolve conflicting messages, and compose new messages based on their experience, perceptions, and judgments. Managers interpret the messages they receive by placing them in the context of a host of other factors, such as strategy, capabilities, upcoming events, personalities, likely reactions of other people. Judgment is required to interpret messages coming to the manager and to craft messages he or she sends out. Thus, the manager adds value to the message. This processing is not typically rule-governed and therefore cannot just be handled by the computer.

Further, much of the content of information in management is not readily put into numbers or text. Much of the information managers receive and process comes through talking with people, either face-to-face or on the phone. In fact, studies show that what managers do for most of the day is talk. About every ten minutes, the manager's phone rings. Critical information is often contained in the body language and voice tone of those with whom the manager speaks. Some issues are too secret or sensitive to be openly stated. Weighing and balancing these different types of information requires a human being. Much of the manager's full appreciation of the meaning and significance of the words being used hangs on his or her assessment of people and their personalities. Because managers manage people and organizations buy from and sell to people, the crucial data is often the emotional reactions of people. Likely support of and opposition to many options has to be inferred. Will department heads cooperate with the new quality improvement program? When the accountants say they will support your proposal at the management committee, will they really? Are the sales representatives genuine when they say they are not considering quitting for another job? Managers are all the time listening to the emotional undertones in conversations, checking body language, and listening to inflections in the voice.

Further, the manager has to put his or her own credibility on the line during these conversations and signal his or her reaction, including use of the right voice tone and body language. Managers not only make statements but try to persuade, cajole, encourage, caution, express distance, and so on when they talk. Managerial communication is always embroiled in an ongoing political process and human drama. Computers cannot play much of a part in this crucial aspect of human communication. They can't detect the nuances in the signals they receive, and they do not have the wit and judgment to implant subtleties in what they send. This subtle and complex process has not yet been captured in a formula that can be programmed into a computer—and is unlikely to be in the foreseeable future.

Of course, middle managers are not simply acting as communicators within the hierarchy, they are also making decisions and exercising their authority in order to relieve the strategic apex in a large complex organization from being overwhelmed by detail. This, in turn, means that much less information needs to flow to the top of the hierarchy than it would if all decisions were centralized. Without middle managers present to filter the information flowing up the hierarchy, the top would soon get buried under the torrent of upward-flowing communications.

Computers are not capable of taking over the information transfer, the information processing, or the decision-making functions presently performed by managers. Since computers cannot take over the core role of managers, they cannot replace managers—though they will continue to assist managers and replace some of the clerks who push paper. Therefore, hierarchy will remain in large organizations.

THE CASE FOR HIERARCHY

The case for hierarchy goes beyond rebutting the four most common challenges to hierarchy as myths. Hierarchies have proven their value over thousands of years and across a multitude of organizational types. Hierarchy was used in the Roman army and then in the Catholic Church for almost two millennia. It has proved to be robust. Consequently, large corporations both in the West and in the East have used and continue to use multilevel organizations as the main mechanism for conducting their activities. The claim that Japanese firms do not use hierarchy and formal structure extensively, and that their success is founded on some other management approach, is wrong. The reason is that hierarchy plays a vital and effective role in coordinating the work of thousands of people in diverse locations. Properly designed, a hierarchy allows people in organizations to combine their different talents and abilities so that the whole is greater than the sum of the parts. Moreover, the concept of hierarchy is neither rigid nor static, and can be varied to reflect today's environment and opportunities, such as greater use of outsourcing and more involvement of employees in decision making. Each of these points is discussed in turn.

Origins of Hierarchy

Almost all armies have adopted hierarchy, even in the newest and most avowedly democratic nations. Armies that refused to adopt hierarchy suffered the same fate as the ancient Britons under Boadicea, their great female warrior leader. The tightly disciplined Roman legions under their hierarchical command structure faced the vastly larger British horde. The British were fighting on their home ground for the independence of their island. They were enthusiastic but lacked hierarchy and organization. In the ensuing rout, most British casualties were sustained through Britons being crushed to death in their confusion. The only way to successfully defeat an aggressive invader who is organized hierarchically is to organize one's own defense forces into a hierarchy for clear command and control. For this reason, one observes the paradox that democratic nations, such as the United States, maintain armed forces that are proudly hierarchical. The American republic attained its independence by overthrowing the British with an army of the people that was organized hierarchically under General Washington.

Like armies, the most successful early corporations were also hierarchical. Alfred Chandler, the renowned Harvard business historian, has described the beginnings of the modern hierarchical American business organization in the railroads of the mid-nineteenth century.[12] Previously, business enterprises were small, such as the shop or trading house that served a local area. However, railroads began to spread their tracks across larger and larger areas as they created a transportation system. This required organization on a far larger scale than previously in civilian organizations. Large numbers of locations, people, locomotives, cars, and freight items had to be coordinated—a complex administrative task. The solution was to set up basic units of track 50 miles long, each internally coordinated by a command hierarchy. These basic units were in turn coordinated by an overarching managerial hierarchy of the railway company. With this structure, it was possible to eventually span the continent with an integrated railroad service.

Chandler charts how this hierarchical organization spread through American business as each industry moved from small to large scale, through telegraphs, retail stores, processed food, steel manufacturing, automobile production, chemicals, oil, and so on. With the expansion in the scale of the enterprise, the original founding entrepreneur and his children were usually replaced as managers by professional managers who were not part of family dynasties. A similar development occurred in Germany. This led to the establishment of what Chandler terms managerial capitalism. The large enterprises at the backbone of modern capitalism are run by professional managers arranged in hierarchies. This system has gradually replaced other forms because it is more effective. In particular, the main alternative organizational form around the turn of the century was the loose federation of companies in a trust or holding company—what today might be called a highly decentralized, flat organization—that failed to manage the units in the group in an economical way. These loose federations proved ineffectual and short-lived, giving way to hierarchically organized corporations.

Chandler found that in Britain, major companies remained as family-run federations, with each child becoming head of a business unit that was run as a personal fiefdom.[13] The failure to establish a hierarchy of command unifying the enterprise, and the resulting lack of coordination, led these British companies to lose out to more hierarchical, effective American and German competitors, ultimately leading to national economic decline.

The historical facts of the birth of hierarchy in the large modern business corporation are a vital lesson. Those who are ignorant of history are condemned to repeat it. Loose federations and family-like firms have been losers, not winners, in the long run. Those seminar instructors who advocate getting rid of hierarchy or who so gleefully turn the organizational chart on its head are mostly appallingly ignorant of business history. Those CEOs who publicly turn their organizational charts upside down are mostly just bowing before a contemporary whim. This whim is often attributed to "lessons from Japan," where collegiality and collaboration are reputed to be the order of the day. But even in Japan, hierarchy is alive and well.

Hierarchy in Japan

Some of the worrying about high overhead costs and slow decision making originates in the slipping international competitiveness of the United States and other established industrial nations. The loss of markets, initially to Japan and now to other rapidly emerging Asian economies, has led to searing inquiries into deficiencies in Western management. In this climate, the notion that Western organizations suffer an excessive managerial burden, with managers indulging their own interests at the expense of the corporation, finds a ready audience. While Western organizations are suffocating under old-fashioned hierarchies, Japanese organizations are said to be forging ahead by being lean and mean in their management staffing, with highly decentralized structures giving the shop floor considerable autonomy.

However, studies of actual Japanese organizations show a different picture. Japanese organizations tend to have a strong hierarchical structure. There are many different ranks of manager: *shacho* (president), *bucho* (department head), *kacho* (section head), *kakaricho* (subsection head), *sagyocho* (foreman), *hancho* (supervisor), and so on. Each major rank may be accompanied by deputies and assistants. Ronald Dore, the sociologist, found in his comparison of British factories with matched factories in the same industries in Japan that the Japanese factories had taller management structures.[14] There were actually more layers between frontline workers and the plant head in Japan than in Britain.

Japanese management is often portrayed as relying on consensus and participation instead of hierarchy in decision making. However, an investigation by two researchers, Koya Azumi and Charles McMillan, shows that this is a gross oversimplification.[15] At the time of the study, Azumi's father was the head of one of the prefectures (local government divisions) in Japan and that helped Azumi obtain the cooperation of 50 Japanese factories in a detailed study. The study examined the degree of decentralization of decision making in each factory. The Japanese organizations turned out to be more centralized than comparable Western organizations.

The hierarchy, however, was combined with the Japanese

practice of participation. The distinctly Japanese cultural device for participatory decision making is the *ring-sho*. The lower-level manager discusses his idea and then formulates it into a written document, called the *ringi*. The lower-level manager then submits the *ringi* to his immediate superior for approval, which is done by adding the superior's seal to the document, like a signature. The document then travels up the organizational hierarchy and across departments, gaining other seals from higher-up bosses until it returns to the originating lower-level manager. That manager now has authority to proceed and take action, for his idea has been approved. This is a system that combines bottom-up participation with centralized control; it combines consensus with hierarchy.

In short, the Japanese have not followed the flat structure trail. They use hierarchy and structure more than many Western counterparts, though hierarchy is combined with participative processes. Moreover, Japanese organizations continue with the symbols and trappings of hierarchy, as any visitor to Tokyo can observe. In the morning, in the lobby of your hotel in Tokyo, you sit waiting for your guide. At the next table sits a *bucho,* heavy with sleep and probably a hangover. He is flanked by two junior managers. They pay court, pushing the ashtray under his cigarette; they are smiling and talking, earnestly seeking to please, and it is not yet 8:00 a.m. Your Japanese guide arrives and you are taken to the main office of a corporation. The reception area is huge and across a vast polished stone floor you are greeted by uniformed and smiling Japanese receptionists who give you a badge and number, identifying you as an entering visitor.

You emerge from the elevator on some upper floor of the corporation into an open-plan office; here are a hundred or so office workers sitting at steel desks in row upon row, a veritable army of administrators. The Japanese guide bows deeply and calls out the name of the person you have come to see: "Inoue, Bucho-san!" Smiling receptionists bow you into a meeting room away from the din of the open office. You sit at a low table with your guide at your side. Green tea is served. Then your hosts enter: the *kacho* and his assistant, the *kakaricho*, a manager from the Personnel Department, another from Corporate Affairs, their assistants, and then the *bucho* and his assistants arrive. Soon there may be six to a dozen people from the Japanese corporation facing you across the table. All of this in a corporate system that supposedly wins by being managerially lean and avoiding hierarchy!

The business visitor will rate lavish gifts and be treated to steak lunches and drinks at the best hotels. At the end of the visit to the corporation, you will be taken by the *bucho* and two or three other managers to the spacious car park in the basement. There the elevator opens out onto a kind of farewelling apron at which sits a limousine, its motor running. Your numbered badge will be removed and you will be ushered into the limo, your hosts waving you out of sight. As the limo turns each corner of the ramp, a uniformed, armed guard will snap to attention and salute you. Hardly a picture of a corporation with no hierarchy or administrative overheads.

The Role of Hierarchy

The Japanese and others use hierarchy because hierarchy is an effective way to direct and control the work of large numbers of people. It is the mechanism that defines who is responsible and the way tasks can be divided and coordinated without continual discussion, negotiation, and readjustment. More importantly, hierarchy allows different kinds of work to be done by people with different skills, perspectives, data, and time frames.

In an effective hierarchy, each level adds value to the organization in distinctive ways. The distinguished organizational researcher and consultant Elliott Jaques has developed the concept of "time span of discretion" (TSD) as a way to distinguish between the work of different levels of management.[16] Time span of discretion is the expected time for finishing the longest task so the responsibility for it is resumed by the superior manager. Most jobs, of course, consist of a set of tasks with various completion times. A sales manager may have a letter to write today, a sales call to make next week, and a new market to be developed within two years. The TSD for a given role is determined by the task with the longest completion time. The higher the managerial level, the longer the completion time.

Jaques found a number of discrete break points in the TSD for different levels of management. These break points reflect the demands of increasingly complex work tasks and the degree of cognitive and other skills required:

- Zero to three months (for example, operators producing products or services)
- Three months to one year (frontline managers coaching a team of operators)
- One to two years (unit managers responsible for a production, sales, or development center)
- Two to five years (general managers responsible for an entire production, sales, or development process)
- Five to ten years (CEOs of a business unit with significant discretion about sales, production, and development)
- Ten to twenty years (group executives overseeing a set of strategically linked businesses)
- Over twenty years (CEOs responsible for sustaining and developing a significant multibusiness enterprise)

The sorts of thinking, problem solving, actions, and decisions involved in working in each time span are quite different. Jaques argues that the capacity to work in these longer time frames develops over time, and that the skills needed for each time frame are quite specialized. Operators need to be able to handle common business difficulties—customer issues, production problems, work flows, scheduling—in an efficient manner. Higher-level managers need to extrapolate broader trends, spot discontinuities, find patterns in customer and competitive activity. Each group needs different data and skills to do this well. Senior managers may well "walk around" but this is a minor part of the role. For example, the frontline manager focuses on the product at hand while the more senior manager looks for clues to new opportunities or solutions to deeper problems, such as with the process or technology in place. Similarly, senior managers may well (and should) see customers, but they aren't simply trying to make another sale; rather, they are trying to understand how customers' needs are changing and what might better meet their needs in the future.

Hierarchy thus not only allows work to be coordinated and controlled across large organizations. It also allows work of different kinds and in different time frames to be carried out. Very large global organizations operate in time frames of years and, more commonly, decades. Building a position in Asia, migrating to a new technology, shifting from a production to a marketing or service orientation are all initiatives that take many years to achieve. Developing, deciding upon, resourcing, and then following up these broad strategic initiatives is the kind of work that the top managers in an effective hierarchy do well. This work is quite different from the important day-to-day tasks of producing and delivering high-quality goods and services to customers. Put another way, hierarchies allow work to be tackled at both specific and general levels of abstraction, and for the general and specific to be coordinated.

A number of leading firms are in fact turning back to hierarchy, having tried other methods of organization. A good example is Coca-Cola. Coke was traditionally sold via independent bottlers and distributors, each doing their own thing in terms of price, promotion, and sales. But as buyers such as supermarket discount stores like Wal-Mart and fast-food chains like Pizza Hut and McDonald's emerged, and as product life cycles shortened, Coke found a need to more closely control its sales and marketing. So it began acquiring distributors and combining what were thousands of small businesses operating in a flat, nonhierarchical structure into a few large hierarchically managed organizations.[17] In addition, Coke found that as it became a truly global firm, top-level managers were also critical in coping with development, expansion, and reorganization. In fact, as Coke has moved into Asia and other growth markets, a key issue has been the recruiting and development of managers.

A graphic illustration of the necessity for hierarchy even in a seemingly freewheeling research environment is provided by the story of Arthur, a case known to us personally. Arthur, a distinguished scientist, had just been put in charge of the R&D center of a multinational corporation. In his first days, he found the R&D staff suffering from low morale. At the time, the 20 scientists were divided into two teams, each headed by a research leader who reported to Arthur. Arthur decided that he would abolish the research leader level and instead have all the scientists report to him personally. He believed that this increase in status would cause morale to blossom.

The flatter structure was implemented and Arthur soon became very busy. He had 22 people sending him reports on their projects, requesting guidance and approvals. He also had to act as the interface between each project and the rest of the multinational, with all the attendant traffic of memoranda, circulars, and information exchange. This was an immense amount of work, with many meetings and much reading. Arthur started working 50, 60 and then 70 to 80 hours each week. Eventually, he concluded that he should recreate a level of supervisors who could carry much of this load on delegation. He reinstituted the two research leader roles and reappointed the two prior incumbents to these jobs.

Some Modern Variants

A hierarchy is not the only way to direct and coordinate the work of thousands of people. Other mechanisms such as contracting out work, forming teams, and employee participation are also being used. But, as discussed in this section, these approaches supplement rather than replace hierarchy.

In recent years, firms have found that they can do considerable directing and coordinating by contracting out noncore business activities. Nike contracts out most manufacturing of its sports shoes. McDonald's contracts out supply and logistics of raw materials and packaging. But the core activities—in Nike's case, designing, specifying, and marketing athletic shoes, and in McDonald's case, managing the delivery of consistent quality and service across a huge network—are done in-house through hierarchies. Within these hierarchies people add value in quite different ways. Salespeople at Nike are responsible for specific accounts. At higher levels, managers worry about issues such as how to sell in various channels such as sport shoe stores, general shoe stores, and department stores. Marketing executives design pricing, promotion, and advertising policies and ensure that they are tightly coordinated nationally and, increasingly, internationally. The idea of every salesperson or marketer going his or her own way, all reporting to the CEO and guided only by his vision, is absurd. If there were no advantages in a coordinated and controlled sales effort, Nike wouldn't need a managed sales force but would be better off with independent distributors. Small businesses would purchase from Nike and then market the product. But Nike doesn't sell that way because if it did, there could be no coordinated Air Jordan model campaigns and promotions, no visible and supportive endorsements from high-profile sports teams, no common image or message. This kind of marketing only works if managed with military precision, so that each outlet has the items being promoted in stock and on display when the advertisements go to air.[18]

Increased use of teams is also supplementing, though not replacing, hierarchies. Teams are being used for special initiatives that cut across traditional organizational lines. Two examples are developing a new product in a new way, as Ford did with the Taurus, and cutting production times and costs, as at Motorola and Florida Power & Light. Teams are also being widely used to do day-to-day production and service work. Instead of everyone having a highly specified job, work is assigned to the team responsible for meeting output targets and for making continuous improvements. The team concept has been found to provide flexibility and to be an effective way to tap into the ideas and insights of the work force.

Kodak provides a good example of the advantages of using teams. At the Melbourne Kodak plant, managers were often remote and didn't understand that the work force had developed and was prepared to act on a number of ideas for cutting costs and lifting quality. Removing levels helped get this message through. In one warehouse, for example, management had designed a conveyor system without conferring with what was seen as a "militant" group of workers. Despite a sizeable investment in new equipment, error rates and costs remained high and relationships between managers and frontline workers were brittle. After the structure was flattened and a team approach adopted, a redesign of the equipment based on input from the same "troublemakers" produced dramatic improvements both in tangible performance measures and in relationships between previously antagonistic groups.

With involvement, training, and the availability of data via cheaper, powerful computing, people are learning to work effectively in teams. But the teams are still part of a hierarchy. Procter & Gamble, whose plants are considered leading exemplars of team approaches, still has plant managers and different grades of technicians, and these people work together in hierarchical relationships.[19] Flexibility, empowerment, and self-direction by teams are not inconsistent with hierarchy. Rather, they are ways in which hierarchies are evolving. Managing with teams does not mean teams without any management.

Another proposed alternative to hierarchy is for all decisions to be reached by consensus or voting, as Ricardo Semler advocates in *Maverick*, the story of his turnaround of his family's failing manufacturing company.[20] Semler fully involved his work force, granting them voting rights on any issue affecting the firm, including executive salaries. But what if some people disagree with the results of the vote—must they go along with the majority, and who monitors and enforces this behavior? If the model of organization is everyone for himself, why do large complex corporations exist? Even in a seemingly egalitarian system such as that described in *Maverick*, who controls the agenda and presents the issues for voting? It can be argued that Semler's company is in fact a hierarchy, but that voting works as an 'escape valve,' letting Semler, the unquestioned owner, know when the hierarchy is losing the support of the work force. Semler's voting may in fact be like the Japanese *ringi*, a supplement to, but not a substitute for, hierarchy. Day-to-day work and decisions are carried out in hierarchies, because that is the best way to effectively provide consistent quality to customers. This interpretation is consistent with other models of industrial democracy. A particularly clear description of such an arrangement is contained in Wilfred Brown's book on the British company that he led for many years, Glacier Metals.[21] There, workers elect representatives who decide, for example, on the policy for introducing a new production technology. However, the policy is implemented via a hierarchy, not a flat structure. According to Brown, the hierarchical nature of the executive structure is critical to the success of industrial democracy.

AN EXAMPLE: DANA MANUFACTURING

Whether a hierarchy is tall or flat depends on more than the preferences of upper management. The number of levels needed in the hierarchy of an organization is determined by the size of the organization and the complexity of the work to be done. Each supervisor can look after only a certain number of direct subordinates. The number depends on how closely the supervisor needs to work with the subordinates. Highly trained experts such as doctors or engineers might need little supervision for complex tasks. Similarly, work that can be well specified and for which people can be trained, such as telephone operators, also needs little supervision. Specialization makes each job simpler and easy to learn, and so less in need of supervision, as in automobile assembly. The assembly line also provides machine pacing that further reduces the need for supervision. Conversely, when work is less routine and when learned rules or routines can't be relied on, more involvement by supervisors is needed, as in custom manufacturing. Further, where jobs are physically separated or need careful planning because of intricate interactions, such as in a job shop, the supervisor can cope with fewer direct reports. Thus, several factors determine the span of control. The factors that lead to smaller spans of control are as follows: geographic dispersion of subordinates, more dissimilar jobs, less training, more coordination, and more planning.[22] Thus, the effective span of control varies across different organizations and within the same organization according to these factors. As the number of people supervised increases, a stage is reached where the manager cannot supervise all of them directly. Some of these people then have to be supervised by a second level of supervisors who, in turn, report to a third-level manager. This creates a hierarchy. The larger the number of people to be organized under a manager, the more levels in the structure. Moreover, smaller spans of control mean taller hierarchies for the same number of employees. Even where the span of control is large it will still be finite, and only very rarely above 50, so a large organization will still have a hierarchy of a substantial number of levels.

The way these ideas work in practice can be seen in the example of Dana Manufacturing, referred to earlier. Assuming a frontline work force of 15,000 and a five-level structure, Dana is effectively using an average span of control of seven. Under the model the work force of 15,000 would be directly supervised by 2,143 first-level managers. These in turn would be overseen by 306 managers at the second level, reporting to 44 at level three. The 44 then report to six senior managers at level four who are directly responsible to the CEO at level five. While in practice Dana's structure is not likely to be so symmetrical—some man-

FIGURE 2.1
THREE POSSIBLE STRUCTURES FOR DANA

Levels of Managers	Span of 7	Span of 11	Span of 25
Five	1		
Four	6	1	
Three	44	11	1
Two	306	124	24
One	2143	1364	600
Workforce	15,000	15,000	15,000
Totals:			
Managers	2,500	1,500	625
Employment	17,500	16,500	15,625
Savings:			
Managers	-	40.0%	58.0%
Employment	-	5.7%	5.3%
Pay costs	-	9.0%	8.0%

agers supervise only two or three while others supervise ten or twelve—the average of seven provides a useful overall picture.

Seven seems quite a reasonable span of control as an average—but it is hardly what might be called a radically flat structure, despite the words of the CEO.

We can use the model of Dana to understand the limited benefits and significant risks of seeking to continue to flatten a structure. In Figure 2.1, we calculate the changes in the span of control required for Dana to go to four levels, as the CEO said he would like to do, and then to go beyond this to three levels. The four-level structure is achieved if the span of control is increased to 11. For this to occur, every manager needs to supervise an average of 57 percent more people, clearly a challenging productivity improvement. To go to three levels requires that the span of control be more than doubled, with each manager supervising an average of 25 people. Thus, to flatten from five to four involves a substantial increase in span of control, and to flatten from four to three would involve an impractically large average span of control throughout the organization. For 15,000 nonmanagerial employees to be organized in a structure with four levels would place an intolerable burden on each of their managers, while a structure of only three levels is totally unfeasible. Every decrease in levels imposes greater spans of control, which soon render further decreases unworkable in practice. For Dana's 15,000 nonmanagerial employees, five appears to be the minimum feasible number of levels required in the hierarchy. For a larger corporation, the minimum feasible number of levels would be larger.

The other point that the figure makes is that while flattening the structure eliminates a large percentage of middle managers, it brings only small and diminishing returns in terms of reducing employee numbers. Decreasing the number of levels from five to four reduces the number of managers by 40 percent, and decreasing further from four to three levels reduces the number of managers by 58 percent. Thus, each cut of one level approximately halves the management. However, decreasing the number of levels from five to four saves only 5.7 percent in total employment, and decreasing further from four to three levels saves only 5.3 percent. One can also calculate separately that roughly doubling the span of control from seven to 15 saves eight percent in total employment. Doubling the span again, from 15 to 30, saves slightly less than 3.5 percent in total employment. Thus, each successive doubling of the span produces *declining* savings in total employees.

To assess the impact on pay costs we can use the rule of thumb of salary consultants that each higher managerial level should receive 50 percent more salary than the level below it. Thus, when five levels are cut to four, total pay costs decline by only nine percent, and when four levels are cut to three, total pay costs decline by only eight percent. Despite approximately halving the number of managers through each reduction in hierarchy of one level, the savings in costs is only 8.5 percent on average. If the span of control doubles from 15 to 30, the total pay costs decline by only five percent. These are still only small savings. Since pay costs are only a fraction of the total costs of a corporation, the impact on total costs of halving the number of managers is quite trivial. For example, if pay costs in a company make up only 24 percent of its total costs, cutting one level will produce a total one-time cost savings of only two percent on average. Thus, flattening structures produces small savings in total employment and costs that decline with each level cut and each increase in span of control. At the same time, as fewer employment costs are being cut, larger risks in terms of unsupervised and/or uncoordinated work are being assumed. The organization can only hope that not too much will fall between the cracks! It is therefore not surprising to find that the grand statement "We are radically flattening" is often accompanied by only moderate increases in spans of control—two to three extra people per supervisor.

The simplistic calls for flat structure also ignore the impact of size. To compare Dana, with 15,000 frontline staff, with a typical smaller firm such as Acme employing 400, and to conclude that Acme with three levels is superior to Dana with five levels is superficial. To then argue that Dana should cut out two more levels—that is, increase the average span of control to 25—is to invite chaos. Flattening an organization beyond the capacity of people to reasonably supervise a given number is counterproductive.

Here we are discussing the effects of flattening structure in an organization that retains the same number of nonmanagerial employees. If this number is substantially reduced, levels can be cut without increasing spans of control. However, substantially cutting nonmanagerial numbers is a substantial downsizing that usually entails reducing the volume of activities and hence losing sales revenue and market share. Thus, it would normally only be undertaken when the organization is forced to do so by increasing competition or economic recession. Such forced downsizing is different from flattening undertaken voluntarily in an effort to be more successful, the scenario being discussed here.

There are a number of exciting and promising innovations that are enabling managers to cope with larger spans of control. Better teamwork and self-management, improved information systems that more selectively highlight when a supervisor's help is needed, and the development of work processes and standards increase spans of control and improve the quality of supervision. But even with these kinds of improvements, simple arithmetic shows that hierarchy is essential in large organizations.

CONCLUSION

Asian countries on average are increasing productivity by six percent per annum, and top U.S. firms such as GE and Citicorp have similar targets. The challenge is to use the hierarchy, as the best overseas firms are doing, to drive productivity up year after year. To halve management for a one-time five-percent reduction in employee numbers and a two percent reduction in total costs is madness. The flatter-is-better trail very quickly leads to a wasteland; to reach fertile fields another approach is needed.

To sum up: hierarchy came into being because it produced results that other forms of organization could not. Formal structures continue to be used effectively in leading economies such as Japan's and in leading firms in the West as well. The problems allegedly caused by hierarchy—high overheads, poor communication, excess red tape—are either exaggerated or in fact have other causes. Nor is technology about to replace the real work of management.

Thus, the challenge, given advances in technology, communications, and education, is not to go back to the small firm or the federation of loosely linked units. Instead, it is to make hierarchy work well by understanding how levels of organization can add value. In a properly designed hierarchy, the manager–subordinate relationship is not one of blind obedience, with one person being all-knowing and the other following.

Rather, as Elliott Jaques points out, each person in the hierarchy has a different kind of capacity and expertise and operates in a different time frame. Hierarchy allows these talents to be combined so that the corporation is effective both in the short and longer term.

The often undesirable status and power divisions that impede communications and morale can be dealt with without abolishing hierarchy. Single-status firms with one cafeteria, one parking lot—no reserved spots—and a single benefit plan are now quite common. Similarly, basing promotions and rewards on merit will help make a hierarchy work better. Introducing processes to involve all employees in improving performance can, if done properly, breathe life into a stultified bureaucracy. Formal structures can also be supplemented by special-purpose teams. But these measures are not replacements for hierarchy. Rather, they are introduced to allow the hierarchy to function more effectively. For a large organization containing many employees, hierarchy is essential.

3

ZEN ARCHERY

Zen archery: the practice of archery by completely clearing one's mind, focusing only on the target, and then letting the arrow fly when instinct says it is right. Tom Wolfe used the Zen archery metaphor about management in his best-selling novel about a Wall Street bond trader, *The Bonfire of the Vanities.* How does a trader know when to buy, hold, or sell bonds? Zen archery is the answer—focus on the target (making money) and let intuition or instinct take over, as the Zen archers of old in Japan did when firing their arrows.

Serious writers on management like Karl Weick, the U.S. organizational theorist, put the case for Zen archery more persuasively. Weick tells the story of the Naskapi Indians, a Labrador tribe renowned for their hunting prowess. To learn where to hunt each day, the Naskapi hold the shoulder bone of a caribou over a fire until it begins to crack and then go off to hunt in the direction the cracks point. Why does this work? According to Weick, because "the Naskapi spend most of each day actually hunting ... What they do not do is sit around the campfire debating where the game are today based on where they were yesterday."[1] The lesson for managers is that action is what counts, not analysis or reflection. Since what triggers the action is unimportant—even bone cracks are fine—intuition and gut feel are preferred to deliberate planning because intuition leads more quickly to action.

Its advocates say understanding why or how Zen archery works is neither possible nor desirable. The processes occur deep in the unconscious and allow the emergence of uninhibited talents that are otherwise repressed or distorted by intellectual activity. Zen archery is similar to the "inner game" ideas, which hold that the correct way to do something, whether hitting a tennis ball or managing people, is within us, naturally, and that we perform best by avoiding intellectualizing. Just do it—if it works, great, if not, verbalize what you would have liked to achieve and try again.

Like the "flatter is better" trail, this one also starts with sound ideas. Intuition and gut feeling are important in management, just as they are in other fields. But intuition should not preclude analysis or reflection. In fact, the most skilled intuitive thinkers develop their gut feel from years of disciplined learning and practice, as Herbert Simon, a Nobel laureate in economics, has shown. Simon explained that what is called "intuition" is more often the accumulation of thousands of items of learning, acquired over many years via keen observation and practice.[2]

Advocating Zen archery as the preferred way for managers to act and make decisions is harmful to the development of management as a skill and knowledge-based profession. It is only a small leap from Zen archery to arguments that denigrate the hard and important tasks of professional management. These arguments tend to take four forms, each of which is built on a number of fads that together undermine the performance of large organizations.

- **Management is action.** Management is not really intellectual work. In fact, intellectual activity is probably counterproductive. The essence of management is action, doing, walking about, making decisions on the spot. Good executives execute, they don't plan, reflect, think, or analyze overly long. And if they do, they are likely to become trapped in "paralysis by analysis."

- **Action is based on intuition.** The Zen, rather than a craft or skill acquired over many years of work and learning, is what counts in guiding action. Therefore, what managers need to do is draw on this intuition. They can do this individually by immersing themselves in activity and "going with the flow." Alternatively, managers can rely on group intuition by empowering teams and drawing out the answers to the issues their firms face from the instincts of those on the shop floor or those in the field who interact with customers and suppliers.
- **Technology and common sense are needed, not education.** Since management is just intuition or common sense, there is no need for education and training in management itself. Management education should be abandoned. As the only really intellectually demanding part of corporate management is technology, future managers should be trained in engineering or other technical disciplines.
- **Executives are overpaid.** Because management involves nothing intellectually special or difficult, managers should be paid only modestly and in line with the pay of really productive employees such as engineers.

Thus, the vital and appealing imagery about managers as Zen archers lends itself to assertions and innuendos that management work is overrated and that managers are overpaid. The assertion is that the paper shuffler, bureaucrat, and analyst have taken over and are destroying good companies. What is needed to succeed against top companies from Japan, Southeast Asia, and Europe are more engineers and scientists—real contributors—and fewer "trained managers." The implication is that management is flaky and that professional managers are not fit to be even Zen archers, let alone warrior chiefs.

While there are ideas within these arguments that are important in the practice of management, the ideas can readily be

taken to their logical but false conclusion that, because the intellectual or skill content of management is low, there is no justifica-
tion for developing and educating people in managerial skills and
theories. Again, what looks like a set of fresh and futuristic ideas,
promising beginnings for a new era of good management, becomes yet another false trail, resting upon fad and fallacy.

We believe that the Zen archery philosophy is, in practice, haz-
ardous to the health of any organization and, in theory, unsup-
portable by either logic or research. In the following pages, we
will rebut each of the arguments made in favor of Zen archery.

MANAGEMENT IS ACTION

The first idea from Zen archery is that management is action
and, by implication, not really intellectual work. Who can
argue with the merit of action? After all, executives are supposed to execute, not sit around all day talking, reading, and
drinking coffee. Moreover, the view that management is action
has respectable underpinnings. Studies of what managers do
confirm that because of the pressure to act, the opportunity for
prolonged formal review of options is often limited.

No Time to Think

In a recent book, Robert Eccles and Nitin Nohria[3] of the Harvard Business School describe a number of characteristics of
common managerial situations. Clearly not all management
follows this pattern, but the main elements are certainly familiar. These include:

- "As a manager, you cannot avoid acting." Even not acting or
  not deciding is doing something, and the nondecision will
  be interpreted by others with whom you work. Thus, there
  is continual pressure to "do something" rather than nothing,
  and to act quickly rather than defer decisions.
- "You cannot step back and reflect on your actions." Much ac-

tivity occurs in real time and involves on-the-spot communication and negotiation. Should a subordinate be praised or reprimanded, should a customer be offered a better deal in a tough negotiation? While taking a few moments out in a negotiation is often possible and desirable, there is rarely time for deep study.

- "The effect of your actions cannot be predicted." Many management situations are complex, and even if the same problem arises twice, a manager can never be sure that the same action will have the same effect. For example, attacking a competitor directly may succeed once and then fail the next time because the competitor has changed its view of the situation, or improved its capabilities. On the other hand, managers are always making predictions, albeit implicit and often under extreme pressures. Every decision has within it a prediction of expected outcomes.

- "You do not have a stable representation of the situation." Most of the time, managers cannot and do not see all the facts relevant to the problems they are dealing with, and even when they do, the facts can change quickly.

Given these characteristics of managerial work, the practical opportunities for a manager's reflection and analysis are limited. Eccles and Nohria, and many other people, conclude that effective managers are pragmatic, flexible actors who keep options open and have a good sense of timing. While the preceding description does not preclude reflection and analysis, the exclusion of those activities from the list indicates at a minimum that they are less important than other aspects of the managerial job. With all the other responsibilities, there appears little room for such luxuries in a busy manager's day.

Any Map Will Do

Given the preceding description of typical managerial work, it is easy to understand the appeal of the action fad: good managers don't plan, they act and react. The only merit in planning is as a stimulus to action. The appeal of action is well illustrated in a story of military maneuvers in the Swiss Alps. We are again indebted to Karl Weick:

> The young lieutenant of a small Hungarian detachment in the Alps sent a reconnaissance unit into the icy wilderness. It began to snow immediately, snowed for two days, and the unit did not return. The lieutenant suffered, fearing that he had dispatched his own people to death. But the third day the unit came back. Where had they been? How had they made their way? Yes, they said, we considered ourselves lost and waited for the end. And then one of us found a map in his pocket. That calmed us down. We pitched camp, lasted out the snowstorm, and then with the map we discovered our bearings. And here we are. The lieutenant borrowed this remarkable map and had a good look at it. He discovered to his astonishment that it was not a map of the Alps, but a map of the Pyrenees.[4]

Weick points out that the map may have helped because mountain ranges have common features, making the Pyrenees not unlike the Swiss Alps. But he then asserts that even a map of Disneyland could have helped if it had inspired action, since from action would have come success.

There are, then, two parts to these arguments that management is action. First, management is action because the situations facing managers allow no other choice. The description of typical management situations outlined above excludes the possibility of analysis, reflection, the scientific method. Whether or not these more rigorous approaches are desirable, time and circumstance just make them impossible. The second part of the argument developed by Weick is that reflection and thought per se are not desirable or effective. According to this argument, there is a large element of self-fulfilling prophesy in managerial work. For example, a manager who asserts, "We need to find some new products for this market in order to beat our competitor," and then acts by spending money on new product development is creating the conditions that will lead to success via new products. Whether or not the initial statement or the product development process was based on analysis is seen as unimportant. Again, Weick's evidence is curious. He uses the story of the Naskapi Indians. The analogy is that developing new products is better than debating whether to try new products, improve old ones, spend more on marketing, or lower costs and prices. These choices are either unimportant, or they will flow from the action—though at what cost?

There is no doubt that these arguments touch a chord. Both executives and MBA students react extremely positively to the readings from which we have quoted, and offer few if any criticisms of either the logic or evidence. It is not surprising, then, that the arguments have found powerful practitioner supporters, most prominently Tom Peters and Robert Waterman, authors of *In Search of Excellence* and its now famous prescription, management by walking around (MBWA), which is offered as the cure for paralysis by analysis.[5] Nor is there any shortage of management folklore to supplement the tales from the Alps and the Naskapi Indians. A typical nonintellectual hero would be someone like "Big Al." The Big Al type is an exception in the United States—he runs a successful steel foundry while most other U.S. plants—large, bureaucratic manager-dominated, slow-moving, impersonal organizations—have closed or lose money. What does Al do? He rides around his steel foundry in a golf buggy, exchanging greetings, praising and exhorting the steel workers and middle managers to lift their game. And he paints his plant white so that dirt and waste are more obvious to the work force.[5]

Skunk Works

Another example of the nonintellectual, action-dominated view of management comes from the burgeoning literature on "skunk works." R&D, innovation, and new product or service developments are increasingly important in an era in which time-based competition is prevalent and ideas flow freely between countries and companies. Where do such innovations come from? Not from management in the conventional sense but from skunk works, small teams of eight to ten people headed by a volunteer and given the autonomy to come up with a new idea or product. The style of these skunk works is highly informal. "We ignore all the rules. . . . We're allowed to get away with a lot. We hardly ever write memos here. Procedures still get in the way of the mission of the venture."[6] Skunk works have recently been credited with the invention of the Stealth bomber[7] and with saving the Ford Mustang from extinction by developing a radical new design.

We have no argument with many of the ideas behind skunk works. However, the concept can very quickly turn into a dangerous pathway, one that places the nonmanaged skunk works on a pedestal and misrepresents large, well-managed projects. It may surprise some people to learn that the "skunk works" at Ford that saved the beloved Mustang was actually a team of 400 people who worked for three years, spending millions of dollars. They certainly broke the Ford rules, or rather designed new ones to accommodate working in teams with suppliers rather than going through Ford's arduous bidding process.[8] But to characterize a three-year, 400-person, megadollar development effort as unmanaged is to denigrate the considerable thought and effort that went into *how* to manage such a process better than in the past. No doubt further innovations in the management of R&D will allow even more spectacular design successes in the future. It is the manager's challenge to understand when to use skunk works and when to use larger-scale, organized R&D, and to make the choice on the basis of knowledge and experience.

Alfred Chandler, the business historian, highlighted this point in his recent major work, *Scale and Scope: The Dynamics of Industrial Capitalism.* Chandler explains that successful large firms such as General Electric, Siemens, and Bayer prosper because their top managements are prepared to continually invest in the processes of management and the development of skilled managers over long periods of time.[9] If the oversimplified notion of skunk works is valid, why have large firms continued to exist and prosper? Why doesn't a venture capital industry take over all R&D?

The idea of skunk works is good because it is a way to move forward with respect to innovation. But when the idea is dogmatically applied as yet another contemporary fad and used to denigrate large-scale, planned, and managed efforts it undermines rather than promotes the development of valuable innovations.

The notion that management is action is almost self-evident, and not one with which we wish to take issue. The call for an action orientation is a healthy reminder that executives are supposed to execute, not simply plan and pronounce. The more interesting question concerns what the action is based on, and in particular whether analysis, reflection, scientific method, principles, and study help in choosing actions that succeed rather than fail.

The contention we return to later in this chapter is that action not based on reflection, analysis, or reasons—action that is solely wish-driven or reactive—is unlikely to produce more than average results. The intellectual underpinnings of successful action have been ignored because they are often hard to observe. Alternatively, they have been scorned or derided because they require tasks that are extremely difficult for many people. In contrast, a populist, antiintellectual approach to management invariably draws widespread support.

How Managers Work

Classic studies repeatedly find that managers appear to spend very little time on reflection or analysis. Henry Mintzberg, a leading writer and scholar on management, describes in *The Nature of Managerial Work* how executives ranging from CEOs to leaders of countries work in short chunks of time.[10] The chief executives Mintzberg observed spent about 60 percent of their day in scheduled meetings, and these lasted about an hour on average. The rest of the time was extremely fragmented—desk work for 15-minute stretches, phone calls averaging six minutes each, and unscheduled meetings and tours of about ten minutes each. Mintzberg concluded that management work is mainly a fast-paced activity characterized by brevity, variety, and fragmentation. Managers talk to people most of the day, trading information, nudging decision processes along, and acting as figureheads or symbols for the organization and its values. They rarely plan, decide, or study. But most of these studies seem to have been of the executive at work. Our own observations coincide with those of Mintzberg, with one exception.

Executives who have reached senior positions in fact do considerable intellectual work—reading, reflecting, questioning—in more than 20-minute bursts, but they do it outside normal working hours. Some chief executives we have observed do two hours of such work each day, either at home or in the office before most of their colleagues arrive. Others work at night, taking home copious reading matter that they subject to critical scrutiny. Alternatively, they spend hours on the weekend "talking about the business," that is, developing and testing ideas with colleagues or friends.

This work pattern is hardly strange to a professional whose job is to apply skill and knowledge rigorously and carefully. Doctors of medicine spend most of their day seeing people in 15- or 30-minute chunks, with occasional longer treatments or surgical procedures. Lawyers, especially partners, move from meeting to meeting, handling countless phone calls and interruptions. Hopefully, these professionals are not just "acting," doing and trying before thinking, but are problem solving in real time on the basis of considerable ongoing education and training. The characterization of managerial work as hectic, fragmented, and varied is quite consistent with the professional application of a skill and knowledge base that is learned over many years, and is then improved and honed in practice and through continuing education. Management can be both action and an intellectual activity. The real argument is not about action versus inaction. Rather, it is about the basis of action, as discussed in the next section.

ACTION BASED ON INTUITION

There are a number of possible bases for taking action. Action may be founded on prior book learning. For example, a manager is presented with a proposal from a subordinate to buy another personal computer. Investment theory requires that questions be asked about the benefits, costs, and risks. The manager deliberately assesses each of the factors and then makes the decision. Alternatively, the action might be based on experience. The request is a small one, the subordinate has a good record, and experience has taught the manager that quick approvals in these cases are highly motivating and entail little risk. Another possibility is for the manager to rely on instinct, gut feeling. While unable (and not required) to give reasons, the manager has a strong initial reaction to the request that tells him it is ill-founded. He says simply, "Let's defer this for now, it doesn't feel right and the budget is tight."

In practice, managers base their actions on each of the three approaches: theory or lessons derived from study, experience, and intuition. Nor are these methods necessarily inconsistent. Experience teaches how theories work in practice and so can be a useful part of logical reasoning. And intuition is often an efficient and effective way to capture and apply the lessons of learning and experience, as we will now see. However, those who argue that intuition is more important than study or experience are courting serious trouble. Intuition, and other popular trends such as teamwork, customer feedback, and trial and error, are no substitute for deep thinking and rigorous analysis.

Intuition

The Zen archers, however, on their pathway to management success, seek to elevate intuition and experience above learned theories or ideas. Ross Perot's comment to students at Harvard Business School exemplifies this approach: "I tell them that I give HBS an A-plus for the young people it attracts, but an F for what it does to them while they're there. 'In due course you'll shrug off this experience and go out and be successful.' . . . By this time I have their attention. The gist of my speech is that if they don't come out of school and get dirty, they won't learn the skills they need to become intuitive managers."[11]

A more extreme version of Perot's argument is set out in a recent article in *Management Review*, which cites "landmark studies" correlating business success and intuition: "At the New Jersey Institute of Technology in Newark, N.J., parapsychologist E. Douglas Dean and engineer John Milhalasky spent a decade studying the relationship between executive intuition and profitability. They asked CEOs to guess a 100-digit number randomly generated by computer. Indeed, 80 percent of the executives who scored above average in intuition had also doubled company profits in the last five years."[12]

The idea behind studies like this is that intuition is something magical and mysterious, independent of intelligence, learning, and analysis. In fact, research tells us exactly the opposite. Leading scholars such as Herbert Simon have shown that intuition is not independent of analysis, but rather complements it. Simon showed that "genius" is often the accumulation of pieces of learning that are piled on each other to build a superior base of knowledge. For example, he explains that chess masters cannot memorize random patterns of pieces on a chessboard any better than novices. However, when the pieces were set up in a form that was part of a game, the masters could memorize the board at a glance while the novices could not. Simon concluded that chess masters knew, that is, had learned, thousands of possible game situations.[13] Their genius was not feeling, intuition, or Zen-like action but deep knowledge supplementing great talent. Similarly, over long periods, top-performing managers learn to see patterns and consequences such as, "If I approve small, seemingly riskless decisions that trusted subordinates care about, they will generally work harder to prove my confidence in them was well founded." When the subordinate asks for the new personal computer, the "intuition" that causes the manager to say yes is really a rational process that compresses prior learning. Moreover, the prior learning may well have been aided by formal study of organizational behavior that also encouraged the trust-based response.

However, Perot-type comments that management is all about experience and intuition and not about analysis or learning are seductive to managers who are frustrated by their attempts to find rational order in the messy situations that confront them. Consequently, the intuitive approach, the Zen archery, is the foundation of a number of popular formulas for supposedly successful management.

Many business gurus prescribe teams as the answer to most operational problems, while others recommend "ask the customer" as the universal solution to marketing or strategic issues.

Teams

Teams, groups of people assigned to work together for a limited period on a defined task, are increasingly common in large complex organizations. As tasks arise that cannot comfortably be handled within the formal structure—a new product or service launch involving manufacturing, sales, and support or a new system crossing geographic or functional units—a team is formed. The best teams act faster and more decisively than the existing organization. They have a goal, similar to winning in sports, and go for it with dedication and enthusiasm. In *The Wisdom of Teams*, Jon Katzenbach and Douglas Smith describe one such high-performance team, formed to establish an intermodal (road/rail) freight service for the Burlington Northern Railroad around major hubs in the northwestern United States, to replace rail services that had previously operated out of hundreds of small depots:

> Following the successful hub pilots, nothing stopped this powerful team. When finance refused to give them an existing cost model with which to build a pricing structure, the team "borrowed" it. When they could not get much needed information or computer support to construct an intermodal profit and loss statement, the team violated company policy and got their own personal computers. When they needed communications equipment to stay in touch with each other and the expanding hub network, they circumvented the communications department and bought voice mail. The team played fair, but by their own rules. And rule number one was "whatever it takes to achieve performance."
>
> Burlington Northern had a long-standing practice of maintaining a low profile in the press; Intermodal advertised heavily. To appeal to truckers, they consciously, and to the rest of the railroads heretically, excluded trains from their ads. Everyone in the industry painted their cars white; Intermodal ordered theirs painted green. They lined up first to try out every piece of new equipment, including one time when they ordered trailers not yet approved by the Interstate Highway Commission.
>
> In one of the many phrases that had special meaning to the team, Dave Burns summarized all this activity by describing what he calls the "Jesuit principle" of management: "It is much easier to ask for forgiveness than for permission."[14]

There is no question that this approach was powerful and beneficial to Burlington Northern. But the story underestimates what was the critical decision for the railroad: to cut out depots and consolidate freight in intermodal hubs. Before proceeding to implement the intermodal system, the team had to convince the chairman and president that the idea was sound. They spent months preparing their case to convince the top executives to approve a pilot test. Yet the descriptions of why the team was successful focused on the team dynamics and composition—the Zen—more than on the analysis, knowledge, and application of scientific problem-solving methods.

This analytic side of managerial work is not only hard for the person doing it but also more difficult for outsiders to write up and appreciate than the attractive idea of "form a team and let them at it." Days collecting data from complex and often inflexible computer systems don't lend themselves to action-oriented prose. Stories about the building of models that don't work properly before the economics of the decision become clear are hardly compelling reading. And, like many managerial initiatives, it is almost impossible after the event to know what contributed most to its success.

Take again the Burlington Northern intermodal hub strategy. What was most critical? Was it team composition and dynamics, or the careful, detailed analytic work that identified which 22 hubs were required, the skills needed to manage them, the necessary equipment, or how the hubs would be advertised and marketed? The folklore tends to emphasize a team acting intuitively and energetically on the basis of experience and dedication. The facts may well be something more akin to the work of scientists or engineers designing and testing a new invention. But who wants to hear about the logical flaws, statistical puzzles, or misleading data that chewed up endless nights and weekends? To tell managers they ought to act on intuition and that teams are the way to do this may be about as helpful as telling a bridge builder to "let the design flow from within," physics be damned. In short, a sound basic idea—teams—unwittingly becomes misrepresented as part of the case for Zen archers.

In fact, the preoccupation with teams ignores research findings that much of a team's effectiveness rests on the expertise of its most skilled member. Team members do not all have the same skills, experience, or ability. Some will be better able to tackle the problem at hand than others. One test of the value of the team is to pit the team's solution to a problem against the solution that the most expert team member comes to alone. This was done in a classic study using the NASA moon survival test. Subjects were told they had crash-landed on the moon with all but 15 pieces of equipment destroyed. The task was to rank the items in the order of their importance to survival on the trek back to base. NASA experts provided a correct list against which answers were scored. It turned out that the groups that simply left the task up to the member with the most scientific knowledge of the moon came up with the best solution. Such groups were better at solving the problem than groups that obtained a representative set of views from their members and conducted intense group discussions.[15] Despite this research, a number of trainers continue to use the NASA moon problem in group dynamics training to prove the superiority of teams!

These findings don't mean that teams are useless, or that they don't bring energy and initiative to tasks that can't be performed by one person acting alone. But the findings do show that learned expertise is important, and that collective intuition—mass Zen—is no solution to tough management problems.

Customers Have the Answer

Another example of instinctive management is the substitution of the watchwords "Just ask the customer" for careful and rigorous market analysis. No one can argue with the principle that asking customers what they want or need is important. But merely asking, listening, and then acting represent a dangerous oversimplification of marketing. Research shows that customers often find it hard to give the real reasons why they do or don't buy, and often may not be aware of their subconscious motivations. Moreover, their reactions to ideas for potential new services or products are extremely unreliable. What an intuitive manager hears are off-the-cuff reasons that are often the customer's rationalizations for past decisions. To make marketing decisions on this kind of information is fraught with danger.

There is another aspect to the denigration of controlled research and analysis in marketing. No breakthroughs, it is asserted, come from market research. According to this line of attack, research might confirm the marketer's intuition but by and large is a waste of money: fashion gurus like Charles Revson, founder of Revlon, and Diane Von Furstenberg, the designer of the Wrap Dress, know intuitively what consumers want.[16] IBM didn't tap a demand for computers: by designing and selling computers, IBM put its concept in place.[17] Through their imagination and forcefulness, these companies created or unearthed a demand that had been unknown and unmet.

Most of these anecdotes about marketing intuition come from writers with little direct knowledge of marketing. But they feel quite comfortable asserting the low value of analysis on the basis of a few cases. That there are as many, if not more, cases of failure from the solely intuitive approach is never mentioned. Who wants to read about failures? Moreover, the fact that consumer goods companies like Procter & Gamble and Kellogg or industrial firms like Philips and General Electric have distinguished records of market success underpinned by careful research is beside the point.

Customer reactions provide a sound first order of understanding of markets that ought not be ignored. But second and third orders of understanding, which require analysis and reflection, can also be vital. The breakfast cereal market is a good example. Many cereals, especially those for children, are quite sweet. If asked, health-conscious parents might consistently say they are worried about the effects of the sugar. What would be the answer? Lowering the sugar content would be a first-order response, but this could lead children to push their parents to buy another brand. Deeper study might show the buying criteria for breakfast cereal to be more complex. Parents could also be concerned about the energy content of breakfast—getting the children off to a good start in terms of food intake; they might also worry about fat and cholesterol. Consequently, a better response would be to keep the sweetness, change the product's message to one about energy (versus taste), and make it look brown, chunky, and wheaty rather than white and sugary. This kind of initiative—though obvious after the fact, like all good ideas—takes considerable research and only comes about because managers are prepared to go beyond the simple first-order customer response.

Customers may well have the answer to all marketing problems, just as genetic structure may have the answer to many medical problems. However, people readily accept that cracking the genetic code takes sustained, rigorous effort and analysis: no one argues for Zen geneticists! Nor are there serious arguments put forward in favor of Zen engineers, Zen lawyers, or Zen scientists. Yet somehow, when the subject turns to management, people lose their faith in using discipline and rigor to crack the tough problems.

More Than Trial and Error

There is a more basic argument against the application of Zen archery to management action. That is the argument of experience. Why do we think that intuitive trial and error, guided by limited and often biased observations of the results, is likely to improve the practice of management when this approach has not worked in any other area? Significant progress in fields as diverse as medicine, science, engineering, and computing did not occur until researchers moved from simple trial and error to more disciplined measurement and problem solving. Even in sports, the best coaches are not simply facilitative psychotherapists—cheerleaders and motivators—but careful students of technique and method, measuring, filming, and then fine-tuning athletes' skills.

Elliott Jaques has argued that management is at about the same stage of development today as the natural sciences were in the sixteenth century. At that time, much of science was in the hands of highly skilled practitioners who learned from the results of their experience and passed on their knowledge to apprentices. These practitioners lacked three things: measure-ments of what was happening as opposed to observations of what appeared to be happening; the ability to deal with dynam-ics and rates of change in addition to statics such as height and weight; and a structure that could join together their concepts and measures. Jaques cites two examples, shown in Figure 3.1.[18]

Where is management in terms of measurement, the ability to deal with dynamics and a structure of knowledge? By and large, management is still a trial and error process, a primitive discipline, often achieving trial and error-type results—with sustained success eluding most managers. Approaches such as Zen archery that ignore the managerial process ("We really don't need middle managers, just give us more technicians!") or denigrate its potential intellectual basis are unlikely to lead to improved results if managers just use trial and error. Crude trial and error, the development of "knowledge" from imper-fect observation and the application of this knowledge by intu-ition, has rarely served mankind well. Why should manage-ment be an exception?

FIGURE 3.1
THE RISE OF THE SCIENTIFIC METHOD

	Old Method	New Approach
Chemistry	Chemistry and metal forming were in the hands of the alchemists—highly skilled practitioners who worked without the benefit of measuring instruments or a sound theory.	The invention of the thermometer transformed alchemy into scientific chemistry and metallurgy within 50 years—by making it possible to know at what temperature given reactions and changes would occur, making prediction and control possible.
Medicine	Medicine was practiced with no real understanding of anatomical structure: bloodletting was thought to change the balance of the humors—the fluids of which the body was believed to be composed.	Vesalius and the anatomists accumulated knowledge of the actual structure of the body—from this foundation, modern physiology, and hence modern medicine, could grow.

TECHNOLOGY AND COMMON SENSE, NOT EDUCATION

Our discussion leads us to the third implication of the Zen archery idea. If management is just intuition, or inspired common sense, then formal education in management may stultify and so harm rather than help prepare managers for their work. The only formal education that is useful for managers, therefore, is in the "real" intellectual disciplines of engineering and the like. America, and Europe to a lesser extent, turns out increasing numbers of MBAs and decreasing numbers of engineers. Japan and other Southeast Asian countries do the opposite—few MBAs and increasing numbers of engineers. The East is succeeding in terms of economic growth, while the West is declining. To those who hold a Zen archery view of management, the connection between these facts is compelling; value is created by technical people, not managerial types, and to the extent that management is needed, the Western concepts taught by leading business schools are wrong. Michael Schulhof, president of Sony Software, made the point in an article in *Scientific American:*

> My experience has convinced me that a background in pure science is an ideal preparation for business. I will take that a step further and say that American business would be a lot better off if it had more scientists and fewer MBA's running its corporations.[19]

A similar point was made by Andrew Grove, chief executive of the Intel Corporation, when advising college students on preparing for a career:

> Study as much of the exact sciences as you are capable of—math, statistics, biology—it doesn't really matter which one. . . . All the sciences give you the logic that you will need. You must do that if you are interested in leading a productive and therefore remunerative existence for the next 50 years.[20]

These views have respectable antecedents. In 1980, Robert Hayes and William Abernathy wrote a much-cited article in the

Harvard Business Review, "Managing Our Way to Economic Decline." In this article, they documented the relative decline of
U.S. productivity and the U.S. loss of leadership in many high-
technology industries over the past 15 years. The reason they
gave was the short-term orientation of U.S. managers, and
their failure to gain industry experience or hands-on technological expertise. Why the preoccupation with the short term?
"Since the mid-1950s," the authors wrote, "there has been a
rather substantial increase in the percentage of new company
presidents whose primary interests and expertise lie in the financial and legal areas and not in production."[21] Moreover,
companies increasingly hire top managers from outside their
own ranks, spurning those with long-term careers in the firm.

The arguments for technology and against management are
not made lightly or without any facts offered in support. And
the arguments have a positive and constructive aspect, as do
most thoughtful challenges, since they are forcing continual
evaluation and improvement in Western approaches to management development and training. Almost all leading MBA
programs are in the throes of review and redesign largely because of the sustained claim made over the last 15 years that
when it comes to management, the West has got it wrong. In
many firms, "manager" is becoming a dirty word, being replaced by "leader" or "coach." "We need more leaders and
fewer (or no) managers" is the popular catchword. McDonald's
wants "crew leaders," not managers. Frank Blount, head of Tel-
stra, the Australian telecommunications company, says his organization of 70,000 or so people needs 70,000 "leaders." Others
call for more intrapreneurs or entrepreneurs. And it would be
best if these leaders or intrapreneurs were engineers and scientists by training, untainted by any study of management.

However, Schulhof's and Grove's argument is not as compelling as it may appear. Research shows that large U.S. corporations run by CEOs with backgrounds in finance outperform
corporations run by CEOs from manufacturing and other
functional backgrounds.[22] And many successful firms are

seeking out people with nontechnical backgrounds as prospective managers. Microsoft, for example, sees a liberal arts education as providing a skill critical to modern management—writing and communication.

Moreover, it is wrong to conclude that Asia and countries such as France and Germany that place a high premium on technical education do not also value and seek to develop management as a professional discipline. In these countries, management and the development of managers is an extremely serious business, but the approaches followed are different.

For example, in Japan, managers are generally developed over a lengthy, largely in-house process that begins with recruitment from top universities such as Tokyo, Waseda, or Keio. The new graduate in an industrial firm like Sumitomo will be assigned to one of two streams, technical or administrative. Employees stay within these streams but are rotated to different jobs every three or so years. Engineers shift between R&D, production, and engineering, while administrators move between marketing, planning, accounting, and personnel. Rotation, the core development process, is accompanied by semiannual evaluations, as well as training.[23]

On-the-job training is now on the rise in Japan, with over 80 percent of newly assigned managers in larger firms receiving basic management training and 80 percent of middle managers receiving further management development training. The topics covered in Japan are quite similar to those taught in Western business schools. Strategic thinking and communication skills are covered in the in-house programs at Bridgestone, the Japanese tire company, and marketing, pricing, promotion, sales forecasting, leadership, and performance appraisal at Sumitomo-3M.[24] In contrast, newly industrializing countries like Korea have a far younger cadre of managers than the Japanese. Many Korean managers are U.S.-educated and are being developed in a way more typical of the United States than Japan. Even within the West, there are a host of different approaches to developing and educating managers. The

French recruit from elite universities and have a management cadre clearly identified at the recruitment stage. German firms appear to be more like the Japanese, with technical and administrative streams in which managers are identified and developed via rotation, appraisal, and training.

In leading firms in all these countries, management is taken seriously, and the skills needed are recognized as requiring considerable education, training, and experience. In fact, a study of four pairs of companies, one in each pair from Britain and one from Japan, found that similarities between management development by industry were more marked than is often suggested by oversimplified claims of cultural difference. For example, the study showed that development of both Japanese and British managers in retailing and banking was quite similar. The implication is that to manage in an industry requires knowledge and skills acquired and developed in ways that transcend generalizations about national differences, such as that the Japanese always hire highly educated technical people and develop them on the job via experience.

These conclusions are reinforced by systematic studies of major Western firms that find that management is an essential ingredient to their success. Alfred Chandler's work, in particular, found that over long periods of time, firms such as General Electric in the United States and Siemens and Bayer in Germany were able to outperform British competitors such as Mather & Platt and British Dyestuffs because of highly developed skills in building and operating management systems for marketing, production, and logistics.[25] How were these advances in management developed? Not by any quick-fix or generic solutions and not by technology alone. In each case, the British invented and had access to the core technologies. Rather, success was founded on years of careful study, experiment, and creative investment in what Chandler calls managerial enterprise. In other words, these firms created integrated organizations with carefully defined structures to allow them to take advantage of the economies of scale and scope offered by new technologies. In fact, one might conclude that the process of developing the managerial enterprise was not unlike that followed by scientists in asking questions and testing solutions or explanations. Putting down management directly or characterizing its essence as Zen archery won't produce these kinds of results, but professionalizing management in the best tradition of science, law, medicine, and the humanities may do so. Perhaps top Zen archers also practice hard and experiment with different equipment and methods. Perhaps there is more to their success than telling each other to focus on the target and to "let the force be with you."

OVERPAID EXECUTIVES

This brings us to our fourth point. The denial of the intellectual side of management makes it sound straightforward and so deserving of only modest pay.

If management is really quite simple—Zen archery and nothing more—and if technical skills are the true source of wealth creation, then technical people should be paid well and managerial types poorly. In fact, pay patterns in the West are exactly the other way around. Zen archery devotees see this as yet another sign of Western decay. To the Zen archers, the alternative argument—that managerial work is hard and that the talent to do it well is scarce—is unthinkable. They point not only to the high compensation of managers versus technical people, but also to the high pay of U.S. managers versus managers in other parts of the world.

The relatively high pay levels of senior executives in large U.S. firms is well documented. For example, according to a survey by Towers Perrin of chief executive compensation in the 50 largest Japanese industrial companies, managers earn an average of about $US873,000 per annum, about one-fourth the pay of comparable U.S. executives.[26] Similar comparisons can be made with other countries. For example, in 1987—the year of the great stock market collapse—the head of the European oil company Royal Dutch-Shell earned $500,000. The head of the American oil company Exxon, of a similar size and with a similar range of businesses, earned $5,500,000.[27]

These high compensation levels reflect the prevalence of incentive pay arrangements that are increasingly common in the United States. Such schemes are rare in Japan, Germany, and most other countries.[28] For example, in 1990, John Sculley, head of Apple Computer, earned $16.7 million, of which $2.2 million was salary and bonus while the rest was the product of a stock-based incentive plan. Similarly, Michael D. Eisner, who is credited with turning Disney around, received $32.6 million in 1988 from stock options, but nothing from this incentive plan in 1989 and 1990.

The trend is increasing in the United States toward higher CEO pay based on big incentives. In 1995, CEO pay at large companies increased by 23 percent. While base pay rose only 4 percent, bonuses rose by 39 percent and stock options grants by 45 percent.[29]

One result of these trends has been a relative devaluation in the pay of engineers and frontline workers. As the Stanford economists Paul Milgrom and John Roberts wrote, "In 1980 the relative pay of CEOs, engineers, and factory workers were all in about the same relationship to one another as they had been 20 years before: All three figures had increased about three and a half times over the two decades. In the 1980s the pay of the engineers and factory workers grew at essentially the same rate, whereas that of the CEOs grew four times as fast. Direct performance pay now accounts for the bulk of compensation for CEOs of large U.S. companies, with annual bonuses contributing 25 percent and long-term incentives accounting for 36 percent of total compensation."[30]

While many people today are convinced that managers are overpaid, we should beware of reaching conclusions too quickly. For a start, managerial pay reflects the amount of responsibility the manager is shouldering. And large U.S. corporations tend to be bigger than those in countries such as Japan and the United Kingdom—because those countries are smaller in population than the United States. As we have seen, much of the pay of U.S. executives criticized as excessive comes from bonuses and incentives. These schemes have been adopted in U.S. corporations to stave off the perceived problem of managers lacking incentives that align their interests with those of stockholders. The pay schemes are not handouts but rather intentional motivational devices designed to reward handsomely for high corporate performance. These financial incentives involve executives accepting a greater degree of risk than they do when they receive a flat salary. The riskiness of senior managerial positions in the United States was traditionally significant because of the practice of firing executives if the corporation performed poorly, rather than guaranteeing lifetime employment. Insecurity increased in the 1980s and early 1990s with the orgy of boardroom coups and CEO sackings. While the total effect of all these factors in determining fair pay for managers is somewhat unclear, it would seem premature to conclude that U.S. managers don't deserve high salaries and bonuses.

The Zen archery school ignores these factors. Its answers to the problem of management in the West not performing as well as it might compared with the East is to pay managers less, and to train them not in management but in science or technology. That way they will spend less time on management and more on technical or product issues. When managerial problems arise, give them short shrift because management is not important—rely on gut feel. Management as such is worthless, or at least not worth nearly as much as it is paid. That current pay levels may reflect a competitive market for scarce talent is explained in terms of the market's being wrong, or as another instance of the perverseness of markets in general.

We see this as a possibly dangerous conclusion, and not unlike the reactions in the past to other new areas of skill and expertise that threatened established orders and beliefs, whether in medicine, science, or manufacturing. We offer an alternative explanation—that the West, in pioneering management as a professional discipline, is building a long-term advantage, but there are inevitable learning costs and growing pains. Hence, we are not surprised to see "mistakes" being made in management, even after careful study and deliberation. These mistakes—bad loans by banks, new products or services that fail, organizational designs that don't function—are not evidence that managers are overpaid and poorly skilled. Rather they illustrate, first, that it is easier to judge decisions with hindsight than at the time, and second, that management as a profession is still evolving and will continue to do so for the foreseeable future.

The Zen archery trail is not only false, it causes damage by undermining the worth of the work managers carry out. Societies tend to value work with significant intellectual content or a high level of skill or craft. Scientists, engineers, legal and medical specialists and researchers and professors are valued because their work requires them to acquire a deep knowledge of an area, and to apply this knowledge via rigorous thinking and analytic activity. We may not fully understand what these people do, but we know it takes an unusual brain and careful application and hard work, and we value these factors. Alternatively, writers, artisans, craftsmen, entertainers, and designers are valued because of the high level of their skill, acquired through years of disciplined practice—often via apprenticeship, service with other master craftsmen, or long and lonely periods of trial and error. Again, we may not fully understand the nature of the skill, but we know it does not come easily, requiring both talent and application.

Conversely, if we want to denigrate a type of work, we attack either its intellectual or its skill bases, or both. For example, the simplification of computer languages has led to a downgrading of programming because "anyone can do that now without much training." The Zen archery pathway embraces both of these attacks with respect to management.

CONCLUSION

In short, Zen archery may be a great way to fire arrows, and following cracks in bones may be a great way for indigenous tribes to hunt for game. But there is no evidence that management should follow Zen-like intuition. On the contrary, reflection, analysis, and intellectual activity are in our view critical as the bases of effective action and reliable intuition. Empowering teams will not substitute for expertise, whether in the team or outside it. Asking customers can mislead unless the questions are properly framed and the answers skillfully evaluated. And while no one doubts the value of engineering or science, those fields are not the same as management, nor is training in these disciplines any guarantee of managerial success. The lessons that are drawn from such attractive but misleading analogies limit the development of management. The common view of management—as relatively low-worth, action-based, intuition-based—is rarely stated in these blunt terms. But that is where this false trail leads, and society as a whole is the loser.

Even the Zen archers admit that, from time to time, management throws up problems for which the solutions demand rigor and application. However, their way to handle such situations is not by tackling problems from first principles over long periods of time. Instead they turn to the third trail, resorting to quick-fix techniques, the subject of our next chapter.

4

TECHNIQUES FOR ALL

Ricardo Semler knew he needed to turn his family's manufacturing firm around. "My colleagues and I tried various
quick fixes for our floundering organization, from suggestion
boxes to leadership training to Japanese-style Quality Circles in
which a range of people from the same business unit, from jan-
itors to executives, would sit down together to find solutions to
common problems. I tried all the prepackaged ideas I could
find, scouring every damn business book with a title that began
with a 'How to . . . ' or ended with the word 'System' or
'Method.' I read Alfred Sloan's *My Years with General Motors*
and Tom Peters' *In Search of Excellence.* I studied popular
business writers such as John Naisbitt, Peter Drucker, Alvin
Toffler, and Robert Townsend, and academic ones, such as
Kenichi Ohmae, Marvin Minsky, business writer Ichak Adizes,
and Henry Mintzberg. I had two bookcases full of business
books, each floor to ceiling. I also sought out executives at
other companies, grilling them about management styles over
lunch. I picked up plenty of ideas and techniques, but I just
couldn't make them work in our offices or factories. Our people would be motivated for a while, but then slip back. I began

to suspect that Semco's problems went deeper than I had realized."[1] Management by technique—the approach that Ricardo Semler tried—is extremely common.

It is preoccupation with technique that we brand as the third false trail. This trail is littered with fads, including yesterday's packaged solutions, like T-groups or management by objectives, and today's prescriptions, like reengineering and value-based planning, which are already showing cracks. Management by technique is a dangerous false trail, as Semler found. Management techniques are not effective management, any more than surgical techniques are successful surgery or sports techniques are winning performances.

Much more is needed. In particular, managers must first ensure that the technique being considered fits the situation. You don't use total quality management to solve a short-term cash flow problem. Second, managers must be prepared to customize the technique so that it reflects the language and operating mode of their organization. For example, some firms tackle problems by working with concrete examples—a defective product, a potential new order, or a letter from a customer—while others focus more on processes and accountabilities. The way in which a technique is applied must reflect how the organization most naturally works. Third, managers who expect results must be prepared to stick with the technique for years and not expect miracles in weeks or months.

However, otherwise skeptical and intelligent managers often seem unable to resist one of the most appealing sales pitches available: "I can help you solve your problems without much effort or pain: it is really quite simple if you buy my technique." The advertisements in airline magazines illustrate this point well: "Learn effective negotiation in two days." "Write insightful plans by plugging in our software." "Become a dynamic leader by listening to our tapes while commuting." Moreover, the sales pitch continues, the cost of the technique—usually hundreds or thousands of dollars—is trivial compared with the multimillion dollar problems large firms typically face. Managing by following a technique is like painting by numbers—each part of the picture is numbered; you just dab in the color the number represents.

There is nothing inherently wrong with techniques. After all, techniques are defined approaches for carrying out activities. Prescribed techniques make activities easier to learn and easier to complete well. We rely on techniques in areas as diverse as adding a column of numbers (carry the tens), business writing (make an outline, set out the points and reasons, give an example) and tennis (hit the ball in front of you, bringing the racquet up and over the ball).

But techniques are also dangerous. Sometimes they limit thinking and flexibility. For instance, at times it is better in business writing to start a document with vivid examples and draw out the point later on, even if in general the technique of ordering by point, reason, and finally by example is usually best. At other times, techniques can be quite wrong because they oversimplify the situation, leaving out considerations that turn out to be critical. For example, modern manufacturing techniques emphasize the importance of operating with "zero inventories," with supplies and components delivered to plant locations where they will be assembled or worked on "just-in-time." But when delivery systems are unreliable and outside the effective control of the manufacturer, a "zero inventory" technique can be disastrous, leading to stop/start operations and high costs. Many companies establishing operations in China, where infrastructure and reliable supply chains are underdeveloped, are relearning this lesson at great expense. The zero inventory technique may work for some components but not all, and one of management's jobs is to understand where and when it might help rather than hinder production. Moreover, applying a zero inventory policy requires detailed systems support and training programs that managers must design and install.

Techniques then are potentially both constructive and destructive. On the one hand, they allow work to be done more easily and at a higher standard than if no techniques were available. On the other hand, they can be like snake oil cures—offering promises that won't be kept since the real situations require discretion, judgment, customization, or analysis that the technique either ignores or brushes over. Unfortunately, many management techniques fall into this second destructive category. Despite this, their appeal is enormous because they address problems that are real and pressing, and because they promise a way into the problem that makes sense. But they often fail because at the end of the day it is not the technique but rather a careful, disciplined, and professional customized application that solves the problem, and the techniques invariably underestimate and undervalue this aspect of management.

In this chapter, we assert that management by technique has become yet another false trail that is undermining the development of effective professional management. A number of the most popular techniques are examined:

- **Planning shortcuts,** including matrices as substitutes for judgment and analysis, value-based planning as the way to bring the stock market to the shop floor, niches as the answer to everything.
- **Total quality management,** especially where it is used more as a formula than as a way of exposing and solving critical problems.
- **Business process reengineering** as corporate USA's only alternative to closing its doors and going out of business.
- **Benchmarking,** supposedly the world's "best practice" as an alternative to critical reexamination.
- **Gainsharing** and other incentive structures as *the* solution for low work force motivation.

Each of these techniques has some merit. Our point is that the techniques, while often useful thought starters or catalysts for action, are *not* management, and that management by technique is an abdication of the essence of management. Managers need to be familiar with techniques, and to adapt and apply them when appropriate. But this adaptation and application is rarely simple and straightforward, as Ricardo Semler

found. Good techniques help managers to lift their performance and that of their firms. Techniques don't substitute for
management, any more than techniques in sports substitute
for training, effort, and skill, all of which the manager needs
too. The promulgation of a technique as "the answer" represents a corrosive and subtle attack on effective management
that should be clearly recognized and rebuffed.

PLANNING SHORTCUTS

There are two decisions that executives have to make whether
they like it or not. Not making either of these decisions is the
same as deciding to continue along the current paths. The first
of these decisions is in response to the question, 'Where should
we compete?' That is, what businesses and product lines or
services are we committed to, which ones will we seek to develop, reposition or withdraw from, and over what period? The
second decision results from the question, 'How will we compete?' Given our businesses, product lines, and services, how
will we carry on activities in ways that are better than those of
our competitors? Will we be more efficient, and provide lower
prices or a greater number of attractive peripheral services, or
will we offer better quality and greater speed and reliability? In
addition, how will we manage our people and assets to ensure
these customer benefits are actually provided—to use the ver-
nacular, how will we "walk the talk?"

Strategic planning was developed to help managers make
these decisions. By drawing on a wide range of ideas from
fields such as economics, accounting, marketing, psychology,
and history, strategic planning offered ways to frame and attack these decisions systematically rather than relying solely on
gut feel or resorting each time to the first principles of logic.

Strategic planning is not the only way to make the "where to
compete" and "how to compete" decisions. Quite often, these decisions evolve as managers live in a situation, talk with colleagues
and customers, soak up the details, and suddenly gain an insight.

Moreover, the decisions are rarely made as single, one-time events, but instead build into a pattern as experience is gained. For example, Brian Quinn, Buchanan Professor of Management at the Amos Tuck School of Business Administration, Dartmouth College, in his classic description of logical incrementalism, described how IBM gradually escalated its development of and commitment to the 360 series of computers—the line that underpinned IBM's success for many years.[2] IBM did not adopt the 360 strategy as the result of some technique. A number of basic studies of technologies, markets, and costs, as well as hands-on experience, finally produced the strategy that was so successful for so long.

Similarly, Microsoft's development of the Excel spreadsheet to compete with the market-dominating Lotus 1-2-3 was characterized by a series of decisions made over time.[3] Lotus was available only for IBM-compatible machines. Microsoft was strongest on Macintosh but had no spreadsheet for IBM standard machines. Initially, Microsoft decided to write a spreadsheet program, Excel, for the IBM standard to attack Lotus in its area of strength. Six months into the project, Bill Gates, Microsoft's CEO, learned that Lotus was aiming a new competing spreadsheet, Jazz, at the Macintosh and switched course away from the IBM PC market, deciding to make Excel the best spreadsheet possible for the Macintosh only. This decision was helped by the realization that Lotus was going to be very hard to attack directly in the IBM PC market until graphical user interfaces such as Windows were more common. Years later, with the advent of Windows, Excel was adapted for the IBM PC format and gained significant share. The strategy that addressed where to compete (spreadsheets) and how (graphical user interface) resulted from a series of research analyses and decisions, and could have been changed at many points.

Decisions such as these are tough to make. At Microsoft, the Excel development started with a three-day retreat convened by Bill Gates that included senior managers and programmers. This was followed by papers, analytic work, and debate. Techniques may have helped frame issues or focus discussion, but it is hard to see how they could have substituted for the sustained effort and thought that the strategic planning required. Yet strategic planning is an area where purveyors of techniques seek to offer shortcuts to thinking deeply and exploring a situation fully, such as by using matrices, focusing on valuation, or proposing universal solutions such as "go for market niches."

Matrix Magic

The business portfolio matrix is a strategic planning technique that seeks to answer the question, 'Where should we compete?' It is based on the principle that 'a business with a strong competitive position in an attractive market is worth investing in. Conversely, a business with a weak position in an unattractive market should be disposed of, closed, or scaled back.' Clearly, it is hard to argue with guidelines expressed in such sweeping and somewhat vague terms. Consequently, it makes sense to combine these ideas in a "four-box" matrix that solves the strategic decision of where to compete. The now familiar Boston Consulting Group matrix does just that.

FIGURE 4.1
BOSTON CONSULTING GROUP BUSINESS
PORTFOLIO MATRIX

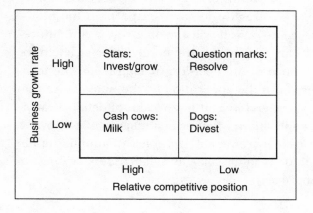

From this matrix sprang many variants, all of which served a useful purpose but none of which addressed the essence of the strategic decision faced by a particular manager. The matrix is useful because it poses good questions—am I in a good industry and do I have competitive advantage? However, the matrix often yields the wrong answer. Suppose you were part of the Microsoft team deciding on whether to invest further in spreadsheets. The market was growing rapidly, but Lotus was dominant. Your competitive position was weak, but your skills in product development were good. If the matrix were applied to Microsoft's position in spreadsheets, Microsoft would be classed as a "question mark." It is quite likely that the matrix, if applied by a team of managers who viewed the spreadsheet market more negatively, would have suggested what in retrospect could have been disastrous—that for Microsoft, spreadsheets were a "dog" and should be divested given Lotus's dominance and Microsoft's own limited position.

More critically, the matrix is unhelpful in answering the key questions of industry attractiveness and competitive positioning. For example, what makes an industry attractive? Is it simply market growth (Boston Consulting Group's initial contention) or a wide range of factors such as profitability, entry barriers, types of demand and customers, and regulation. If a wide range of factors is to be considered, how are they traded off? Even more importantly, can one assume, because an industry has been unattractive in some respects in the past—whatever this means—that it will stay that way in the future? Similarly, how can future relative competitive strength be judged? The essence of the decision making is *not* the technique, the matrix, but the application by the manager of reasoning, imagination, and insight to a wealth of detail. Strategy formulation is application, whether in a major study or over a period by a series of incremental decisions. To limit this application to technique is to trivialize and denigrate a key part of the managerial process.

Valuation is the Answer

The matrix also fails to deal with a key concern of managers in public companies, namely, whether the strategies followed are creating value for shareholders or whether the company is becoming a takeover target. To quote from a recent book by consultants Tom Copeland, Tim Koller, and Jack Murrin from the McKinsey Corporate Finance Practice:

> Many of the popular frameworks for *corporate strategy* suggest that the key to success is picking the right mix of businesses— that if a company has a balanced or diversified portfolio of well-managed businesses all will be well. That is an appealing vision, but it is too narrow; it overlooks entirely the need for corporations to manage value. . . . The essence of corporate strategy is to figure out how the corporation, as intermediary, can add value to the business it oversees.[4]

The answer is to apply a valuation methodology that discounts projected cash flows for each part of the business and for each decision made within the business. Value is added when the firm is able to obtain a greater stream of cash flows than other owners. Where this is not possible, the way to create value is to sell to a more suitable owner.

Again, as with matrixes, there is no quarrel with the idea. The problems emerge when the idea is translated into a technique that is simplistically applied. The valuation of cash flows from a business or part of a business is trivial. Any numerate high school student who can play on a computer could generate the answer with all kinds of sensitivities (for example, "If sales are ten percent higher per annum then value is doubled"). A top university student, better able to grasp the financial concepts being used and more articulate, would be positively dangerous. She might well argue to managers in charge of the business, "You *must* accelerate sales growth ten percent per annum because otherwise you will halve what would have been the value of your business." Whether or not this higher rate of sales growth is achievable, and at what cost in terms of possible competitive reaction, would be brushed over. Nor is the judgment that another owner could increase cash flows an easy one. The skills that this new owner is supposed to bring always look better from a distance, and in any event, there is no guarantee that the potentially better new owner will pay a price premium that reflects their superior skills.

The point is that the valuation is the end of the process, and represents a framework for tying assumptions and projections together. The hard part of planning is to generate the assumptions and projections. Turning again to Microsoft's Excel initiative, how might these cash flows have been estimated? The potential trap in these kinds of techniques is that, while they appear clinical and objective, they hide what are inevitably subjective judgments. Champions are not always objective, and managers need to balance enthusiasm with realism in deciding whether the projections are reasonable. The McKinsey valuation text, in discussing these kinds of difficulties, concludes with the somewhat Delphic comment: "Consult a text on strategy analysis for a complete analysis of factors that should be considered in developing scenarios" on which the projections of cash flows will be based.[5]

Finally, the valuation school is quite divided on what is the best or most correct way to value an investment. That "cash is king" and that "discounted cash flow return on investment" is the appropriate basis for valuations are far from clear. New research is highlighting the need to consider other approaches such as option pricing theory. This is designed to deal with the reality that in most businesses there is a range of possible new initiatives being considered—a new product or product twist, a different way to deliver a service, a new technology, a new relationship with a potential partner, supplier, or customer, an acquisition. Some emerging businesses are no more than sets of such possibilities. At some point in time, cash will have to flow if the possibility is successful, but projecting the timing and

FIGURE 4.2
OPTION PRICING APPROACH

	Stock Option	Business Opportunity
Price of option	Set in options market	Cost of R&D and preproduction to bring idea to market
Time to exercise	Established in option contract	Window of opportunity given likely competitor actions
Expected value of exercising option	Range of possible values for stock based on past price volatility	Range of possible values of investment based on best estimates

amounts of cash is nigh-well impossible. Thus, other valuation techniques such as option pricing are being considered. The possibilities are valued as if they were options on opportunities.

Figure 4.2 compares those parallels between valuing a stock or share option and valuing a business opportunity. The investment needed in, say, R&D and preproduction is the price of the option. The time available to exercise the option is the window the company has to go to market given possible competitor reactions. The potential value of the option is a probability distribution of the payoff if various scenarios occur. These factors are then combined in a pricing formula, and the value of the option can be compared with the cost of acquiring it via R&D, preproduction, and similar expenditures. Again, the option technique does not deal with the same underlying problem faced by other valuation approaches, namely, what are the possible scenarios, how likely are they, what could be done to make them more attractive? The answer ultimately is in the application of basic reasoning and substantive judgment, not in the technique, however helpful it may be in presenting the "right" solution.

Niches Are Nice

Another common strategy assertion consistent with both the matrix and valuation methods is that companies should seek and find a "niche." The idea is that in tough markets, especially today, when many firms are feeling increasing competition, it is possible to avoid head-to-head competition by finding a niche. The aim of a niche strategy is to identify a market segment that has few, or preferably no, competitors and serve that market segment by means unavailable to competitors. Thus, the niche is a kind of walled garden in which the firm can bask undisturbed in the sun. The niche strategy is implemented by withdrawing from the broader, less profitable markets that suffer from destructive 'head-to-head competition' and concentrating resources and attention on the niche market.

The technique has proved highly persuasive. The problem is that there is reason to doubt the validity of the assumption that niches exist and, especially, that if they exist they will endure across time. Thus, the central plank of the niche technique is open to question. The key issue is whether there exists a wall around the garden.

For many years, the niche strategy and its earlier form, product differentiation, were taught in business schools by reference to the example of automobile manufacturers. The story told was of how mass manufacturers such as Ford and General Motors had established successful large-scale businesses based on low-price, mass-produced automobiles. However, these were vehicles for the masses, and there was an up-market segment of customers who looked for superior vehicles and were able to pay a higher price. This luxury market was a niche containing superior manufacturers who made fewer vehicles with less mechanization and more handwork and who sold to the discerning customer at a higher price that covered the higher manufacturing cost. Niche marques included Rover, Triumph, Jaguar, Riley, MG, Alfa-Romeo, and SAAB. By 1996, every one of these firms had been taken over by a larger mass automobile maker (e.g., Jaguar by Ford and SAAB by General Motors). None of these smaller automobile companies making superior automobiles for the elite market segment has been able to remain independent. Their niche markets have not generated reliable

profits and have not allowed sustained growth as indepen-
dents. The automobile business has turned out to benefit from
large-scale production and from capital investment and lower
costs. These, in turn, have allowed product development, particularly in engines and production process improvements,
which has allowed mass producers of inferior cars such as the
Japanese to steadily improve to the point where their products
compete in increasingly upper-class market segments and
command increasingly high prices.

At the time of this writing, even Porsche is beginning to feel the
effects of Japanese competition and is losing out in sales (though
the strong German currency plays a role here). Porsche is interesting because, while its original strength was product engineering, it has recently played a strategic marketing game such as
stressing the investment value of its high-price automobile in consumer advertisements. The company reinforces this strategy by
not allowing dealers to discount and by taking back surplus stock
to forestall discounting. But the recently declining sales suggest
that customers are mainly interested in acquiring a car for their
car dollar and seek other outlets for personal investment.

Japanese automobile manufacturers have used their asset
base of large volume and large research expenditure to create
a range of increasingly sophisticated products: powerful luxury sedans such as the Toyota Lexus, sports cars such as the
Mazda RX7 and MX5 (Miata), and true exotics such as the
Honda NSX. The Rover sedan range now includes cars that in
engine, mechanical parts, and basic body are Hondas. The
British element is increasingly restricted to the interior trim
details, such as walnut fascias and leather seats, or the finer
points of the suspension settings. Thus, as regards the upper
segments of the British car market, there has been no real, sustainable niche. The Japanese mass producers have entered the
luxury product market. The previously independent firms have
lost their coveted independence. There is no wall around the
garden. There is no effective Keep Out sign against the relentless forces of competition.

Not only is the niche market strategy of questionable validity, but there are signs that the niche strategy may damage those who adhere to it. A comparison of the U.S. and Japanese electronics industry illustrates the point. In a recent study, William Egelhoff of the Fordham University Graduate School of Business found that U.S. firms had gradually moved out of hardware production and had come to concentrate on software.[6] U.S. firms had made both software and hardware until Japanese firms began to produce the more generic hardware and drove down the price. After analyzing these market segments, the U.S. firms found them to be poor profit opportunities. They withdrew from production of these generic devices, ceding the market to the Japanese. The Japanese then entered the market for more sophisticated devices and drove down their prices. The U.S. firms again analyzed these market segments and found them to be poorly profitable given the head-to-head competition. The U.S. firms therefore withdrew from production of these more sophisticated devices, ceding the market to the Japanese. Eventually, some of the U.S. firms withdrew totally from the production of hardware devices and now concentrate solely upon producing software.

At every step in the process, the U.S. firms followed the rules of the niche technique: analyze market segments for differences in profit and exit from competitive, low-profit market segments to concentrate on areas where there is a comparative advantage and thus the prospect of earning high profits. However, the new niches proved as vulnerable as the old niches before them, and after a few years, competition broke out in the erstwhile secure zone. The culmination of this process of withdrawal based on immediate profitability criteria was that some firms had exited an entire industry and category, that is, hardware production of a class of electronic devices. Egelhoff cites the widespread withdrawal of U.S. firms from the DRAM segment of the memory market during the latter half of the 1980s.[7] Worse yet, there were indications of synergies between software and hardware businesses such that vertically integrated

Japanese firms enjoyed a systemic advantage over their U.S. rivals, with potentially grave consequences for those U.S. firms in terms of their profitability. According to Egelhoff, pursuing a trajectory of successive concentration based upon a search for highly profitable, less competitive market segments through strategic analysis has been injurious to U.S. firms and to the whole U.S. industry. Yet this is precisely the decision process that would follow from persistently pursuing a niche strategy. The walls close in every few years until the garden is the size of a tomb. If, instead of following the simplistic niche strategy prescriptions, the firms had concentrated on serving customers better through constantly improving hardware and software and finding complementarities, many U.S. firms would at least still be in the market.

THE QUALITY JOURNEY

Planning techniques trivialize one part of management work: the making of major commitments with respect to the future of the organization. Other techniques, particularly when taken to their extreme, trivialize the tasks of day-to-day operations and improvements. The most prominent operational technique is total quality management (better known as TQM), as described in Figure 4.3.

TQM began when teams of workers applied math and statistics to understand where and why business processes were causing faults or errors. If deliveries are late or costs erratic, don't yell at the staff—have them systematically understand the

FIGURE 4.3
TOTAL QUALITY MANAGEMENT

Total quality management is a philosophy, captured in specific processes and values:

1. The achievement of quality, which is defined by customer needs
2. The systematic analysis of processes to reveal the main cause of quality problems
3. The involvement of employees in process improvement

processes that control delivery or cost and then fix the processes. The Japanese adoption of Deming's ideas and the success of high-quality Japanese products, from cameras to cars, is well known and has inspired many U.S. European and Asian Pacific companies to buy into the quality approach. Quality awards now exist in many countries and attract thousands of applicants for what are seen as prestigious prizes. In the United States, the Malcolm Baldrige National Quality Award was established by Congress itself in 1987. Baldrige-winning companies such as Motorola that have embraced and succeeded with TQM are much admired and copied.

We have no argument with the goals of producing goods and services of high quality, of getting things right the first time, of eliminating errors and aspiring to high standards. Nor do we challenge the need for firms to closely reexamine their processes and to look for the systematic causes of errors rather than just chase down and seek to rectify poor-quality services or items after the customer has been served. Our concern is with what is happening as TQM is promulgated as a universal, simplified technique that will invariably deliver these results.

The evidence of companies that have used TQM is on our side. As Oren Harari of the University of San Francisco recently wrote in *Management Review* following a survey of a number of studies on the impact of TQM, "about one-fifth, and at best one-third of TQM programs in the U.S. and Europe have achieved 'significant' or even 'tangible' improvements in quality, productivity, competitiveness or financial returns."[8] The survey conducted by the consulting firm Rath and Strong of 95 Fortune 500 companies illustrates the point.[9] Respondents were asked to identify their most important objectives in introducing TQM, and then to assess whether TQM had a major impact on meeting these objectives. The main reason for introducing TQM was to respond to or initiate a competitive thrust. In 40 percent of cases, TQM helped produce the desired result, but in 60 percent of cases it did not. TQM most directly aids competitiveness by helping firms satisfy more demanding customers (60 percent success rate), which is consistent with its being a quality improvement program. Thus, TQM sometimes delivers positive benefits for firms but more often does not.

How can these results be explained? Some part of the failure of TQM programs to deliver the goods is due to insufficient commitment to working through the application in detail.[10] As we have argued, technique alone is not enough and has to be turned into concrete improvements in the organization, based upon factual analysis of each organizational case. When TQM becomes a technique driven by staff specialists who emphasize form over substance, line managers tend to be unsupportive. The experience of the U.S. utility Florida Power & Light, a leading exponent of TQM, illustrates this point.

At one time during the TQM implementation, Florida Power & Light had about 1900 teams working with the guidance, direction, and support of 85 full-time staffers on TQM projects. Literally thousands of processes, ranging from the replacement of light bulbs to the paying of small accounts, were being methodically examined by teams trained in statistical and process flow analysis. Form and bureaucracy began to drive out substance to the point where the 85-strong staff contingent had to be disbanded. Once line managers again started to work on the application of specific ideas to lower costs or speed up responses to customers, rather than on filling in forms, success was assured. As proponents of TQM point out, when TQM programs fail it is often because management, particularly top management, either implements them poorly or is uncommitted to TQM, refusing to devote adequate time, money, and visible political support to the process.[11] Firms like Motorola in the United States or Tubemakers in Australia, which have succeeded with TQM, have spent more than ten years adapting and refining the simple ideas described in Figure 4.3 for their particular circumstances.

In our view, some of the frequent failures in TQM programs are caused by a more fundamental problem, the promulgation of TQM as a technique that provides "the answer" to very general aspects of management. TQM helps the quality goal, but quality is then overgeneralized as 'the answer' to the quest for productivity and competitiveness. A number of studies purportedly show that firms producing high-quality goods and services achieve high productivity and earn high returns.[12] Quality, however, is undefined, and general statements about the relationships between quality, productivity, and competitiveness are meaningless. The words are too imprecise. They signal that something ought be done better, but what exactly, and how? There are many different aspects to productivity, and it is unlikely that all are equally pressing in a firm at a particular time.

Both corporate strategy and economics recognize at least three types of productivity:

Technical efficiency is achieved where individual firms produce the goods and services that they offer to consumers at *least cost*. Typical measures cover outputs per unit of input, often in physical rather than dollar terms (e.g., units produced per hour or calls per shift).

Allocative efficiency is achieved where the resources needed to produce a set of goods or services are allocated to their highest valued uses (i.e., those that provide the greatest benefit relative to costs). Allocative efficiency is measured in financial terms, such as relative return on investment.

Dynamic efficiency reflects the need for industries to make timely changes to technology and products in response to changes in consumer tastes and productive opportunities. Dynamic efficiency is captured in time-based measurements, such as whether to be first to market with an innovation.

A given firm at a particular point in time is unlikely to have an equal need to improve all three aspects of productivity. Typically, one or another stands out. For example, in electricity utilities where large investments are made in generating and transmission equipment that will be operating for many years, technical efficiency is likely to be critical much of the time. Squeezing every kilowatt of power from each ton of coal, hour of labor, and piece of equipment is all that can be done once a plant has been built. However, when the utility faces a decision to add a new unit of generating plant, allocative efficiency comes to the fore.

Similarly, a bank finding that the spread of automatic teller machines and changing demographics is making a number of traditional branches less viable faces the problem of allocative efficiency. There is little point in improving processes in a branch that no longer has enough customer demand to keep going. Instead, management has to reconfigure its network and decide how to use new technology. No wonder top management in this situation will seem uncommitted to a process like TQM that drives for technical efficiency.

A third case is fashion industries and firms undergoing major change and discontinuity. These will be more concerned with dynamic efficiency, being first and fast. For example, firms that live off "first mover" advantages by leading their competition in the introduction of new products and services are often able to capture price premiums. These higher prices are often sufficient to cover up technical inefficiencies, at least for a time. For example, the firm leading in a fashion line may not be the most efficient at producing a new style of clothes, but may well obtain the lion's share of profits on the trend, as Ken Done, the Australian designer, did with a particular pattern on T-shirts and bags. A process like TQM might help cut waste, but it misses the point of what is critical for these firms. Ken Done's success is a function of rapid innovation, design, and a price premium, not low-cost manufacture. In fact, the Rath and Strong survey found that TQM was quite unsuccessful in decreasing time to market, and none of the 95 firms surveyed said that "improving the level of innovation and initiative" was its reason for introducing TQM.[13]

In short, high-level prescriptions such as "Improve quality to achieve productivity" are rarely useful, and universal solutions have more chances of failing than working. The art of management requires finding a fit between processes, actions, and situations. Techniques like TQM may be a start. But only experienced, thoughtful managers can answer the questions. When is TQM likely to work for us? How should it be applied in my firm? What training and support do we need? What does the firm need that can't be accomplished with TQM?

THE BUSINESS PROCESS REENGINEERING MANIFESTO

As the limitations of TQM have become better understood, the search for the all-encompassing technique takes up a new trail—business process reengineering, also called core process redesign or process innovation. TQM is failing because it is too narrow and built on outdated assumptions according to the reengineers, and thus a new technique is called for. The main ideas behind business process reengineering are as follows:

- The concept, attributed to Adam Smith, of dividing a company's work into tasks that are most efficiently carried out by people who are trained for and assigned only one such task, is now outdated. This kind of thinking leads to the old Henry Ford production lines, where each worker did only one type of job all day. Such thinking no longer fits a more competitive environment in which improved production and information technologies and a more skilled work force require companies to customize, invent, and adapt at great speed.
- Instead, managers should reorganize their firms around processes. A process is defined as a "collection of activities that takes one or more kinds of input and creates an output that is of value to the customer."[14] Thus, fulfilling a customer order, beginning with a request and ending with a delivery and payment, is a process. Assembling the order, shipping goods, and creating an invoice are not processes but tasks, which in a "traditional" organization would be carried out in separate functional units—the warehouse department, the transport department, and the accounting department— often under different managers.
- To reengineer, to reorganize around processes so defined, demands discontinuous thinking, throwing away old assumptions

and beliefs. To quote from the leading exponents of the technique, Michael Hammer and James Champy; "At the heart of business reengineering lies the notion of *discontinuous thinking*—identifying and abandoning the outdated rules and fundamental assumptions that underlie current business operations. Every company is replete with implicit rules left over from earlier decades: 'Customers don't repair their own equipment.' 'Local warehouses are necessary for good service.' 'Merchandising decisions are made at headquarters.' These rules are based on assumptions about technology, people, and organizational goals that no longer hold. Unless companies change these rules, any superficial reorganizations they perform will be no more effective than dusting the furniture in Pompeii."[15]

• Reengineering is fundamentally different from TQM and other forms of continuous incremental improvement. TQM and its derivatives apply at a detailed level, taking the overall processes as given. Thus, a TQM approach to improving order fulfillment might have a team in the warehouse working on how orders can be assembled more quickly and accurately. Another team would examine invoice generation. A third might look at procedures for dispatching trucks. Business process reengineering, in contrast, would study the entire order fulfillment process with one team, searching for a way to reorganize the whole process, possibly making a first- or second-line manager responsible for all aspects of order fulfillment in at least one region.

To managers frustrated by the somewhat bureaucratic and detailed approach of TQM, these ideas sound extremely attractive. Books and articles on reengineering are doing well, and the subject has been 'hot' on the seminar circuit. However, as managers heed the call to reengineer they find something very similar to the experience with TQM. Most efforts at reengineering seem to fail. Even Hammer and Champy's book, *Reengineering the Corporation*, admits as much, estimating that 50 to 70 percent of reengineering efforts fail to produce the dramatic gains intended.[16] Why is this the case?

Few concede that the technique itself may be at fault, though some concerns are expressed about its generality and non-specificity. Exactly what do you do to reengineer? Isn't reengineering just another version of basic problem solving and project management? Isn't it really just a new label for what used to be called rationalization, that is, cutting out unnecessary steps, operations, administrative procedures, and personnel. There are numerous ways to rationalize—computerize, outsource, reform the workplace, and eliminate unnecessary steps: business process reengineering corrals them all together.

Mostly, however, according to the defenders of reengineering, the problems are with poor implementation, usually resulting from an uncommitted chief executive and top team. The main implementation problems are thinking too small, getting caught up in fixing subprocesses from the bottom up rather than seeing the big picture without constraints, and refusing to demand very significant improvements. Lack of commitment is found in executives' failure to devote adequate resources to the technique, assign the "right" person to lead it, and keep reengineering at the top of their agenda. Committed managers must crash through, not drag the process out, and be prepared to make at least some people unhappy.

One of the authors of reengineering has an even more interesting explanation for the failure.[17] The problem of performance cannot be solved by reengineering processes. Instead, what is first needed is a "reengineering of management." And what does this entail? Just follow the ideas set out earlier: flatten structures, abolish hierarchies, operate like a happy family, be action-oriented, use teams, be more visionary and less prescriptive. In short, before using the reengineering technique, run down all the other false trails.

The fact that proponents of business process reengineering also wish to reengineer management points up the consistent strand of radicalism in their worldview. Their language carries a strident tone, with words like "reengineering" and "manifesto." Something dramatic is happening—or should be. This begs the question of whether every firm ought to be going through a radical change in its fundamental operations. Some firms undoubtedly require this. But for many other firms, the requirement is rather for fine-tuning and incremental improvement of what is basically a sound system. Evolution, not revolution, is more appropriate.

Yet the whole business process reengineering (BPR) movement carries with it a conviction that massive reconstructive surgery needs to be visited upon many organizations. This is not a powerful insight into business. It is a questionable presupposition that can easily lead to irresponsible acts of destruction, which are the opposite of good management. Thus, if most reengineering efforts fail to attain the dramatic gains intended, this may indicate a lack of feasibility in the goals set—their intention was too dramatic. The high failure rate of reengineering may reflect the unreality of the expectations that are raised by the heady rhetoric of the reengineering revolutionaries. The problem is less a failure of implementation than a flaw in the reengineering concept, which presumes such grand inefficiencies everywhere. Whereas BPR calls for the reengineering of management, we wonder whether the need is not rather for BPR to be reengineered! The assumption that radical revolutionary change is needed almost everywhere deserves to be challenged.

There is another possible explanation for the many failures of reengineering: reengineering fails because it is seen as a technique that will provide "the answer," rather than as a thought starter for professional managers. There is no real inconsistency between Adam Smith's 200-year-old ideas of task specialization and the new idea of reengineering. Adam Smith was right when he pointed out that specialization was the key to efficiency. It is the application of these basic ideas that has changed, not the idea. We no longer need to or ought to specialize today in the same way that people did in the 1800s. But nor should we throw away the idea of grouping work into sets of activities for which there are specialized processes, knowledge, and skills. For example, instead of specialists in data entry who spend all day punching the same kind of data into a computer, there are now specialists in order fulfillment who do a range of tasks to ensure that customers' needs are met. The reengineering idea is valuable because it raises the question, "Are managers organizing (i.e., specializing) around the right set of tasks, given today's environment?" But it becomes less valuable when it is seen as a technique that offers a simple solution to this age-old question. While techniques come and go, the real hard work of professional management remains. There is no substitute for intelligence, experience, and analysis embodied in the skillful application of ideas.

THE BENCHMARKING MANTRA

Both TQM and reengineering are closely related to yet another surefire method of operational improvement: benchmarking. Benchmarking and the achievement of the world's best practice have almost become a mantra for modern management—the solution to static productivity, inadequate sales growth, or profligate use of assets. The idea is simple: find out what the best performers in the world are doing and catch up, fast. Clearly, this is a powerful and valuable idea, especially for firms in countries like the United States, which has been domestically oriented, and Australia, where distance and lack of competition have left performance in many firms well behind the standards set by the best international competitors. But, like the other techniques discussed in this chapter, benchmarking and best practice have limitations, and these limitations become more severe the better a firm performs.

Benchmarking, put simply, has all the advantages and disadvantages of copying. Thus, where an enterprise is clearly behind current best practice the results of a good benchmarking exercise may be helpful. The disadvantages of benchmarking are obvious for a firm that is already among the best in the world. Put another way, against whom does the leading runner pace himself or herself, and how does the runner know whether or not it is possible to do even better, by a wide margin?

However, benchmarking may be of limited use even if one is only a follower. One reason is that differences in the performance of firms may be due to factors firms cannot control. For instance, in many industries, larger firms enjoy economies of scale relative to smaller firms. Data may show that unit costs of production are 15 percent less for the Acme Company, which is ten times larger than the Brown Company. Brown may set Acme's costs as the industry benchmark, but it won't be able to attain them, because its scale is only one-tenth that of Acme's. For a company like Brown, the Acme cost benchmark is a forlorn hope that is more likely to frustrate and depress its staff than motivate them to find another way to compete against Acme's structural cost advantage.

Benchmarking also misleads when it is mechanistically applied to every activity of the firm. One of the most common failures of benchmarking exercises results from managers trying to compare themselves to others in too many dimensions. They forget the Pareto principle, the well-known 80/20 rule. According to this rule, only 20 percent of factors drive 80 percent of performance. The most critical part of benchmarking is the identification of the 20 percent, usually three to five key success factors. The technique merchants glibly gloss over the thinking and analysis required to identify these key factors. Moreover, benchmarking these factors carefully and thoughtfully takes considerable time and effort.

In the present climate of public anxiety about national competitiveness and ready vilification of management, benchmarking can unwittingly play its part. By erecting "the world's best" standards against which managers and their organizations are to be judged across all activities, benchmarking guarantees that almost everyone can feel like a failure! Since scale and other factors put the world's best performance beyond the control of most managers, benchmarking raises expectations without providing the means to close the gaps identified.

Even where it is feasible for a company to be the world's best, the benchmarking approach runs into another problem—a failure to deal with the unimagined, with innovation. There are countless ways to carry out business activities. No proven theories dictate how best to handle a customer inquiry, produce a quality service or product, or advertise effectively. Business is a rapidly evolving area whose disciplines are still poorly understood and in which prediction is always difficult because the past is an unreliable guide to the future. This idea is elegantly expressed by the distinguished economist Joseph Schumpeter, who talks of the "creative destruction" of markets and competition, as a result of which the unimagined drives out the existing.[18]

The discovery that customers prefer to select their own groceries and other goods revolutionized retail productivity. Benchmarking the shop assistants who served customers from behind counters in traditional corner stores would have thrown little or no light on this opportunity. Similarly, benchmarking a manual production process would be unlikely to generate opportunities for robotics. In short, despite its many advantages, the main limitation of benchmarking is that it focuses enterprises that are behind on catching up by copying, when the real challenge is to find new ideas to get ahead. In so doing, it can lead managers to adopt practices that are in place in other enterprises, rather than to seek what has not yet been imagined or instituted.

These limitations of benchmarking are recognized in many emerging management approaches that draw comparisons between current practice and perfect performance, even where no enterprise has yet achieved this goal. The new approaches encourage managers to set goals on the basis of the best possible level of performance, irrespective of the results of current practice anywhere in the world.

In other words, rather than look at what others are doing, start with a clean sheet of paper and figure out the best performance possible, then set this as the goal. We note that this idea of the highest possible goal is one of the more positive aspects of TQM. For example:

- Instead of accepting competitive levels of defects, strive for *zero defects* in every aspect of work. Errors that cause rework or rejects are to be avoided, and the standard to be aimed at is always 100 percent, irrespective of the achievements of competitors. The same principle can be applied in service areas such as dealing with inquiries and orders, making deliveries, invoicing, or providing credit.

- A related concept, found, for example, at the New United Motor Manufacturing, Inc., plant (NUMMI), the joint venture of Toyota and General Motors in Fremont, California, is that of *zero waste*. Waste of any kind—minor materials, time, paperwork—as well as major items and inventory, is to be avoided.

- Just-in-time production relies on *zero inventories* and consequently on the arrival of work in process at exactly the right place and exactly the right time. These ideas are also applied in service firms, where the aim is no queuing between work stations.

- Programs aimed at flexible manufacturing and service delivery have as their goal an economic order size of one unit, and the *elimination of all delays* in cycle times or customer response times.

- In setting standards for how technology should be used, the concept of the *scientific limit*, or the performance that can be achieved from a given technology without breaking a fundamental scientific principle, is becoming increasingly common. Thus, in converting energy in a power station or steel mill, for example, the standard set is that of perfect energy conversion, allowing only for those losses that are required to carry out the reactions required by the conversion (see, for example, Richard Foster's *Innovation: The Attacker's Advantage*[19]). This is inevitably higher than the design limit, and challenges people at work to go beyond the current design until they hit a scientific limit, such as the melting point of metal in a machine, or the speed of light and the size of an electron in a computing application.[20]

In short, benchmarking and the identification of best practice provide useful information for managers seeking to improve. But the information is often incomplete, ignoring what has not yet been imagined, and the approaches have clear limitations because the essence of benchmarking is emulation, while the essence of successful competition is gaining an edge. Once the benchmarking is done, the real managerial work of invention, change, analysis, and the application of skill and judgment begins—and the technique says nothing of these factors.

GAINSHARING

Another set of techniques has been developed around pay. If only the structure of pay were correct, the argument goes, then people at work would automatically act in ways that lead to company success. Gainsharing, from the chief executives to the front line, is the key, then, to any problems of motivation or retention of skilled people. Gainsharing comes in many forms: payment for each unit of work, each part produced, form processed, or customer served; sharing the gains from productivity improvements; and profit sharing and stock ownership plans.

However, gainsharing rarely turns out to be the great universal solution, though it is an important element in management. There are two main reasons. First, despite the notion that all that really motivates is money, pay rarely comes out as the top factor in surveys of what people are looking for at work. As shown in Figure 4.4, surveys of workers in the United States, Europe, Japan, and Australia indicate that only in Europe is pay ranked as the most important aspect of a job. Other factors, such as pleasant colleagues, interesting work, and a job that allows achievement and matches one's abilities, are as or more important.

The second reason gainsharing flounders is that when schemes seek to replace management judgment by formula, rigidity very quickly causes the formula to become counterproductive. Various gainsharing schemes have been tried, ranging from piecework to team or group rewards to profit sharing across a firm. It is now well accepted that piecework formulas invariably fail. Factors beyond the worker's control—supply of parts, reliability of machinery, a difficult customer—may well lead to targets being missed even though, under the circumstances, the worker has done a superb job. Conversely, luck can produce a dream run for a co-worker in terms of output, even though little was required over the shift. How can these problems be addressed? By managers making judgments that override the formula.

Nor are group formulas any better. For example, consider a bonus paid for factory output that reaches a set target. If there are a hundred workers in the factory, each employee only produces one hundredth of the total output of that factory. Thus, whether or not a worker receives a bonus from the factory, hitting the output target depends upon the other 99 workers. The worker may feel that he or she is working hard to help the factory make its target, but that some other workers are loafing and pulling everyone else down. The first worker may decide to give up trying. Alternatively, he or she may continue working hard and then feel cheated when the shirkers get equal shares

FIGURE 4.4
WHAT WORKERS WANT; THE MOST IMPORTANT ASPECTS OF
THEIR JOBS

United States	Europe	Japan	Australia
1. Pleasant colleagues	Good pay	Job matches abilities	Job allows achievement
2. Good pay	Pleasant colleagues	Pleasant colleagues	Interesting job
3. Interesting job	Good job security	Good pay	Good job security
4. Job allows achievement	Interesting job	Good job security	Opportunity for initiative
5. Good job security	Job matches abilities	Good hours	Pleasant colleagues
6. Job matches abilities	Job allows achievement	Responsible position	Good pay
7. Responsible position	Opportunity for initiative	Not too much pressure	Responsible position

Source: See Hilmer[21].

in the bonus. Some good workers will leave the company. Those that remain may decide to drift down to the mediocre level of their peers.

Economists are passionate advocates of monetary incentives, but even they recognize these "free-rider" problems. The economists' solution is to appoint a manager to make sure that everyone does a fair share. This, of course, supports our case. In other words, monetary incentives have clear limitations that only skillful management can overcome.

Another problem with gainsharing concerns the amount of money paid for performance. For example, share ownership schemes, while helping build an interest in and commitment to the firm, rarely are more than a minor part of a worker's pay packet. A worker on $30,000 per annum would need to hold shares worth $100,000 and returning ten percent per annum for the scheme to really make an impact. And even if the worker were prepared to hold this kind of stake, the relationship between his or her effort and the reward would still be quite tenuous. While there are always stories of spectacular payouts to employees, the reality is that only 35 percent of U.S. firms offer any kind of variable pay to frontline employees, and average payouts per employee are about 7.5 percent of base salary.[22] Moreover, only a small fraction of these firms believe the gainsharing to be highly effective.[23]

Introducing gainsharing is not without cost. Pay for performance puts some pay at risk, whether managerial pay or of any other employee. Pay now fluctuates according to performance, rather than being stable and flat. Economics has long held that risk must yield reward, otherwise no one will accept it. Therefore, companies that ask their managers or employees to bear risk will have to remunerate them at a higher rate on average than companies that do not. Hence, the average wage levels for the same employees will need to be higher in the company with pay for performance. Gainsharing only makes sense, then, where the benefits from superior motivation are greater than the higher remuneration costs.

In short, pay is never a universal solution, and certainly not one amenable to rigid formulas or techniques. The idea of monetary incentive schemes is that employees expend effort to raise their performance so as to earn the reward. Psychologists who have looked into such monetary incentive schemes find that each of three factors must be in place for them to work. Employees must see the connection between high performance and reward. They must also see the connection between their effort and the resulting increase in the performance measures used to determine the bonus or incentive pay. They must believe that expending effort will reliably lead to the reward. Each of these links can easily be broken and can rarely be made simplistically. Employees may not understand the connection between high performance and reward because they do not understand the mechanics of the scheme. They may see too weak a connection between their effort and the increase in the performance measures, because their efforts are diluted by others or because the performance measures are flawed. Lastly, they may not believe that expending effort will reliably lead to the reward, instead fearing that they will be subject to a speedup. If any of these three conditions fails to hold, monetary incentive schemes will fail to motivate employees.

Good managers use monetary incentives. Our point is that they do this not simplistically but rather by tailoring pay to the particular needs and capabilities of their people at particular times. When they seek to avoid these judgments by following formulas, the rot sets in.

CONCLUSION

It was not the simpleminded application of a faddish technique that helped Ricardo Semler turn around his family's ailing business. Instead, Semler crafted a unique approach that fitted his company's predicament at a particular time. The elements of Semler's approach were hardly revolutionary—participation by all employees in all decisions in an environment where the survival of the firm was clearly at stake. Semler made the approach work because of consistent application and experimentation over a number of years. The irony is that the Semler experience is now being sold as yet another quick-fix, universal solution to all the problems of management.

The message for managers from this chapter is to beware of such claims. Planning shortcuts won't replace the judgment and analysis needed to decide where and how to compete. TQM is not a religion that guarantees salvation—it rests on detailed statistical and process analysis by numerate and literate employees able to work cooperatively, and will only address certain types of business problems or goals. Reengineering, with its call for revolutionary discontinuous change, can as easily lead to failure as to success. It, too, is a tool for special situations, and fit and careful application are far more important than the generic technique. The same is true of benchmarking and gainsharing. In short, a set of interesting ideas become corrupted because their advocates lose sight of the fact that success depends not on techniques or textbooks, but on the painstaking application of a combination of customized solutions, usually over long periods, by experienced and thoughtful managers.

Finally, we note that the very idea that generic techniques can be a source of competitive advantage is illogical. In competitive markets, a firm succeeds because in some key respect it is different from other firms. It may have lower costs, better service, more attractive designs, or be easier to deal with or faster to innovate. Firms that do exactly what their competitors do don't earn high returns. If packaged approaches really worked, all competitors would follow the formulas and no competitive advantage would be possible. Detailed application of ideas to the specific circumstances of the firm, however, is something that cannot be mimicked readily. The rewards go to those managers prepared to discover their own trails, not to the followers of fads.

5

THE CORPORATE CLAN

The fourth false trail—creating a corporate clan or tribe—follows easily from the preceding three. What will provide direction, guidance, coordination, motivation, and high standards in the modern high-performance organization? Not hierarchy, for flatter is better. Not analysis or reflection, for management is action and intuition. Not carefully crafted management systems and approaches, for canned techniques will do. The answer is "culture." According to this view, organizations are clans in which members are held together by a common culture of shared values, vision, and symbols. People collaborate through an implicit understanding of what is required, often without even having to put it into words. There is little need for managers, ordering about underlings via memos or verbal instructions.

Like the other false trails, this one too starts with a good idea and then carries it to absurd conclusions. We take no issue with the notion that large corporations tend to develop distinct cultures, and that shaping the culture to enhance performance is an important role of management. Many firms have gained significant improvements by fostering a culture of customer service (SAS), design excellence (Ikea, Cross), innovation (3M, Mi-

115

crosoft), or teamwork (Goldman Sachs). But what starts as a good idea about one of the tasks of management then becomes a quick-fix solution and even an alternative to management. "We don't need managers," the proponents of these fads argue, "we need to act like a clan, inspired by a leader with vision."

In a clan, everyone thinks and behaves similarly. Clan members cooperate spontaneously. The unifying thread, however, is not management or a managerial structure. It is corporate culture, the norms that bind and guide the clan members, such as excellence, customer service, and respect for individuals. Common language, myths, and protocols guide thoughts and actions. "We always use first names." . . . "We dress the same way (whether in blue suits or no suits)." . . . "We are meticulously punctual." . . . "We will shut the line immediately if any worker has concerns about quality." . . . "We place a lot of emphasis on physical well-being and fitness—you won't find fat people in this company." . . . "We are one big team." There are words or symbols whose significance is uniquely understood by clan members. With its vision, language, and protocol, a strong corporate culture develops solidarity among clan members and motivates them in pursuit of common goals.

Given that everyone in the clan is headed in the same direction, the conventional tasks of management become trivial. There is no need for people to be appointed managers with authority over others. Such power and status differences are inimical to the clan's spirit of equality, though leaders, people with vision, are acceptable and even necessary. Marking off territories with boundaries and jurisdictions is also wrong—everyone shares and collaborates informally. The clan view leads naturally to the notion that the organization should be boundaryless, with no internal walls and also no external walls separating the clan members from their customers and suppliers. Customers and suppliers are to be drawn into the community, where the common culture and feeling for one's fellows leads to spontaneous cooperation. The business world becomes a competition between clans, like the Japanese *keiretsu*, the networks of related companies that have existed for many years. Leadership enacted through vision, values, and symbolic behavior replaces traditional management. The yogi replaces the commissar, and worrying about where the buck stops becomes old-fashioned, for it stops with everyone.

These ideas are immensely appealing to those seeking relief from the hard slog of conventional management, and they appear to have strong backers in both management and academia. Jack Welch, CEO of General Electric, declared that his aim was for General Electric to become a "boundaryless organization," with no walls internally or externally. The oneness of General Electric would be a source of competitive advantage. In a similar vein, management writers advocate building a strong corporate culture as the answer to flagging competitiveness, poor quality, and low morale. A key academic book, *Theory Z*, by the Japanese-American professor Bill Ouchi, contrasts the traditional formal American organization with clan-based Theory Z.[1] Japanese organizations are said to follow something like Theory Z, which is key to their successes in worldwide competition.

Ouchi goes on to write about a basketball team in which mutual understanding is so great that formal leadership is absent and "coordination is unspoken." However, he concedes that in a basketball team composed of selfish members the coach has to enforce hierarchy. This is the principle Ouchi applies to organizations generally, that is, that clan rather than hierarchy should be the aim but "frailties" require formal hierarchical structure.[2] He goes so far as to admit that "most organizations" need some formal structure for this reason. Despite this significant qualification, he advocates the development of organizational clans as egalitarian communities of people who work together based on shared goals and an intimate understanding of each other.

Ouchi asserts that clan-type organizations are more effective than conventional hierarchical forms of organization because clan members share the same goals, trust each other, and work intimately over a long period of time.

The ideas of clan and culture are not without merit. Writers on organization, starting with Mary Follet at the beginning of the century, have urged managers to pay attention to the "informal organization"—norms, power structures, and the texture and quality of human relationships at work. Man does not live by formal organization alone. Culture can and does supplement effective organization. But like the other false trails, what starts out as a useful idea quickly becomes an undermining fad, as managers are urged to supplant systematic structures and process with clans and culture.

In this chapter, we argue that the clan concept endangers organizational harmony and productivity. There is plenty of evidence against the value of clan-based organizations.

- Throughout history, clans have rarely been the winners that their proponents claim them to be.
- The Japanese model does not support the clan idea as a central ingredient of Japanese success.
- Leading companies in the West that are put forward as exemplars of the clan-based organization are actually using clan rhetoric and not really following clan principles.
- Becoming a strong corporate clan with a single culture can harm a large complex firm by inhibiting the diversity of its cultures and ideas—the lifeblood of a vibrant organization. Clans may be comfortable, but sustained success often comes from being pushed outside the comfort zone by nonconformists.
- Clans are incompatible with the increasing diversity of work forces in terms of, for example, gender, ethnic background, language, and nationality.
- The darker side of clans and culture is often ignored or downplayed. Clans can and do encourage groupthink, the replacement of independent critical thought by emotional action, at times with dire consequences.

In short, clans and cultures are no substitute for management. At best, they provide a useful way to guide an organization, but in their extreme versions these ideas actually detract from good performance.

LESSONS FROM HISTORY

Neither military nor social history supports the idea that clans are particularly effective. The word clan has its origins in Scotland, where for centuries the clans were the key economic and social units. The McDonalds, McTavishes, and Douglasses each had defined territories, distinctive kilts, and enduring feuds and alliances. England, in contrast, had moved to the more modern social structure of cities, broad social groups, and formal government.

The last great flowering of the Scottish clans was at Culloden in 1746. At the time, the Scots were restive under their English conquerors and sought freedom under their own king. The clans rose and their fighting men came together under Bonnie Prince Charlie, armed with swords and shields though without a system of provisions. The English sent against them a modern army with muskets, amply supplied. The two sides faced each other at Culloden Moor.

The English formed disciplined lines of musketeers, braced for the mass charge of the clans that was the Scots' mode of warfare. The Scots were assembled in clans, but with empty bellies because they had run out of food. The clansmen waited for the order to charge: nobody gave it. Prince Charlie was young, with little military experience. And the clans, each being autonomous, lacked a military hierarchy. Hours went by, during which the English, hardly able to believe their luck, rained shot upon the clansmen, exacting a grim toll. The clansmen chafed at their inaction, and isolated clans charged the English lines but were easily contained by the superior English numbers. Eventually, the English sent troops to fire from the side, so that the clansmen were now raked with fire from two directions.

Culloden was a terrible defeat for the Scottish clans. The victorious English army wreaked destruction on the highland population, helping to end the era of the Scottish clans. The lesson is that clans are no match militarily for modern organizations with advanced technology and logistic flows.

Sociologists studying the evolution of modern societies in

the nineteenth and early twentieth centuries also find a movement away from clans, not toward them. Clans were the key to
the small rural communities in which people once lived their
whole lives. In such rural communities, family ties were all-im-
portant and everyone knew everyone else. Norms were strong
because everyone was constantly being watched by everyone
else. Values were shared because all attended the same village
church and school and so were exposed to the same limited set
of ideas. There was a high sense of community identification. It
appeared that everybody shared the same fate and sense of
purpose. People were enmeshed in a broad set of mutual obligations that applied to economic exchange as well as to social,
religious, and family relationships.

With urbanization, people moved to the cities and lost their
involvement in tight-knit, small-scale communities. People
achieved anonymity in the city. They were free to learn new ideas
from the diversity of religious, political, and other opinions that
surrounded them. They were exposed to a passing parade of differing life-styles and values. Extended family ties were weakened
as relatives were scattered throughout the nation. The family,
work, religious, and political life of the individual were carried
out in separate spheres with different people. Relationships between people were organized around specific aspects of life
such as employment, recreation, and the supply of services and
goods. People in cities had a group of people they knew at work,
groups of friends centered on personal interests, and perhaps a
group of trusted suppliers and service providers. No longer was
there one intimate group that met all needs.

Economic exchange becomes more important as the individual has to buy much of what previously was grown, made, traded,
or given. Transactions turn around price and service, not ongoing
social relationships. The individual is often involved in transactions with large organizations, both private and public. Thus, urbanization and industrialization destroy the old world of the clan
and usher in the world of formal organization and the market.

Given this sociological development, it is deeply ironic that some contemporary organizational scholars such as Ouchi advocate that clans largely replace formal organization and market transactions. This is less a use of sociology than a misunderstanding. There is no turning back the tide of history. It is attractive to fantasize a return to the village green, but it is not going to happen. The cottages around the village green have been sold to wealthy commuters from the big cities. The chatter in the village pub is disturbed by the ringing of mobile phones.

There can be no return of the clans because they have been pulled apart by geographic and social mobility, by urbanization, by the large scale of modern corporations, by work force diversity, and by internationalization. Nor is the situation different in Japan or other Eastern economies.

JAPAN AND THE CLAN

Japan's business successes have often been hailed as strong evidence for the clan model. However, this is an overly romantic view of modern Japanese corporations and modern Japan. Prior to industrialization, clans comprising groups of families occupied different parts of Japan, not unlike in Scotland. As discussed earlier, William Ouchi uses this historic clan image to characterize modern Japanese corporations as adherents of Theory Z. The greater success of these corporations relative to their Western competitors is explained by each corporation's being a clan. Clans are contrasted with the more impersonal bureaucratic structures of the Western corporation, giving rise to the popular idea that in Japanese corporations there is little Western-style formalism, just spontaneous cooperation between clan members and tight adherence to common standards and behavior through strong mores and informal communication. In a Japanese company, all employees know the right way to do things and behave accordingly.

The true picture, however, is somewhat different. Numerous studies, referred to in Chapter 2, show that large Japanese organizations have elaborate formal structures, like large Western organizations. They possess tiers of managers arranged in hierarchies, and tend to make more status distinctions than equivalent Western organizations. They have an equal or greater number of managers than equivalent Western companies. They have as much division of administrative work into specialties, as many rules and regulations, and as much paperwork. The content of their training and education, while delivered differently, has much in common with that in firms in parallel industries in the West. Western audiences have been fed a picture of the Japanese as courteous, harmonious, and caring for each other. Yet in reality they are riven by status differences, competition, and jealousy, just as Westerners are. At a Tokyo cocktail party, the senior manager may snub a smiling manager of lesser status, destroying his face in public. The business card proffered by the younger person may be taken—without the older man's reciprocating with his own. Social death in the big city. The false image of Japanese harmony and consensus provides fertile ground for the myth that Japan's corporations are cozy clans run on mutual vision and culture.

Far from representing some indigenous Japanese culture with origins lost in the mists of time, the structures and management approaches used in Japanese corporations have very specific origins in the industrialization of Japan. Shipbuilding was one of Japan's first heavy industries and its organization was modeled on the Prussian naval dockyards. Later, office administration in Japanese corporations was again influenced by German ideas, in the *bureaugesellschaft* movement. Subsequently, as is well-known, Japanese organization was molded by American ideas, such as Deming's quality management and supervisory training through the widespread training-within-industry scheme.

Japanese organizations have been deliberately created in emulation of the West, for the Japanese, keen for economic development, quickly appreciated the power and potential of "managerial capitalism." In many respects, the Japanese have implemented Western management ideas more thoroughly than the West. As the distinguished sociologist Ronald Dore argues, Japanese corporations are if anything more like Western governmental civil service organizations than clans.³

One way in which Japanese organizations are said to be like clans or tribes and quite unlike Western organizations is in their observance of the job-for-life practice. According to this practice, Japanese employees do not job-hop between organizations, as in the West, but stay at one firm for life. This leads to a stable work force with strong norms and learned common behaviors. However, job-for-life applies only in large Japanese corporations and often only to managers. Most Japanese workers are employed in smaller, less secure companies that supply the large firms on a contract basis, as in the auto industry. Lifetime employment is not granted at these smaller subcontractors. Even in large corporations, some employees are temporary. For example, at Toyota, many assembly workers are from agricultural regions, brought in on five-year contracts and expected to return home at the end of their term. For managers in those companies where job-for-life is prevalent, employment is administered through the much-feared central personnel department, which keeps records on each person, including regular performance appraisals. Even the distinctive elements of the Japanese system are formal and bureaucratic.

In short, the clan model of the large Japanese corporation is not accurate. Large Japanese organizations are actually structurally complex with elaborate formal organizations. They have many managers. Status and hierarchy are more highly developed than in the West. Job-for-life limits movement between companies but means that each person is locked into a civil service-style career system, in which each competes with peers for life. This is not a world of soft-focus harmony based purely on informal communication and shared values. While clan ideas and rhetoric appear strong to outsiders, these ideas are not being used in place of formal structures and processes. Thus, it would be wrong for Western firms to give up formal structures and systems and try to replace them with corporate culture in the belief that they are thereby emulating Japanese success.

The real message of the success of Japanese corporations is not that the West should embrace clan management. On the contrary, Japanese corporations have outperformed their Western competitors because they have more thoroughly and effectively implemented Western management techniques than have Western companies. This is seen, for example, in quality management, low-cost production, and asset management.

MYTHICAL CORPORATE CLANS IN THE WEST

The clan concept has not only been overplayed in explaining the Japanese miracle. It has also been wildly exaggerated as key to the success of a few strong Western organizations. Two somewhat diverse examples, Apple Computer and General Electric, illustrate the point.

Apple

Particularly in the early days under Steve Jobs' leadership, Apple was said to be a culture-driven clan par excellence. Informality, teams, and fun, coupled with strong values and a will to create and innovate, were the order of the day. A video clip often used in training programs advocating a clan approach showed Steve Jobs talking to a mass audience of his employees. The employees had been bused to a large auditorium and were in a party mood. Jobs and other executives talked about the company and its recent success record, reaffirming its core values and mission. Steve Jobs then unveiled the latest Apple product, a new-generation PC. With great panache, he inserted a diskette and strode from the stage. The computer talked to the audience: "Hello, I'd like to introduce my friend, Steve Jobs." The employees cheered. Clearly, everyone had a great time. But is this really an example of a strong corporate clan based on sharing and openness?

What is classified as the new clan-type corporate culture was really nothing more than old-fashioned hoopla and hype propagated by the hierarchy. Sometime later it was announced that unsold inventories were much too high and that Apple was in financial difficulties. The clan-type rhetoric was at variance to the nitty-gritty operating problems. Steve Jobs was replaced by John Sculley, a professional manager from PepsiCo. Is this a clan in which all are treated equally and share a common fate together? The surface rhetoric of shared commitment obscures the ongoing use of hierarchy to stagemanage the rah-rah sessions and to solve the operating problems. Thus it is problematic to say that Apple was a clan organization in which people were equal and cooperated spontaneously based on shared goals without hierarchy.

General Electric

There has been much talk about the recent successes at General Electric being based on a rejection of conventional management, such as planning and formal organization, and the embracing of corporate culture and clan-style management. While the successes are clear, it is not at all certain that they flow from the clan concept.

For starters, Jack Welch, by his words and deeds, has removed much of the sense of stable, guaranteed employment that was characteristic of General Electric. Employees have been declared redundant in large numbers and over 100,000 jobs have been eliminated. Management has stressed that each employee's continuation at General Electric is contingent upon achieving high levels of customer satisfaction and profitability. Any business not number one or two in its industry is to be closed or sold. This message may pervade the culture of General Electric but it is the opposite of the stable, long-run membership of which clans are made. You do not sell your mother because she is not performing. Your cousin does not cease to be your cousin if he slips to number three in his industry. Welch is instituting performance-based market discipline, not clan coziness.

Welch and his chroniclers Noel Tichy and *Fortune* magazine's Stratford Sherman espouse employee participation, empowerment, and involvement down the ranks of the company.[4] General Electric's commendable achievements in this direction are substantial and may well have contributed to its financial turnaround, as Tichy and Sherman claim. However, high employee participation can coexist with retention of central power at the top of the hierarchy. Much is made of the open questioning and give-and-take between managers in meetings at Crotonville, the General Electric management development center. A key event is the question session, in which Welch goes into "the pit" and answers any question put to him. But it is arguable how much this signifies a rejection of hierarchical management in favor of clans. Tichy and Sherman tell of a manager at one of these forums asking Welch about the future of the manager's division in General Electric. Welch replied that he had just sold it that morning! What more vivid demonstration of the power of the center could he have given. It is unlikely that this event readily faded from the memories of those present at or aware of the session. Such changes in the business portfolio at General Electric are highly sensible and have undoubtedly contributed to the turnaround, but they are manifestations of corporate hierarchy, not clan.

Advocates of clan management and corporate culture often also urge leaders to practice transformational or charismatic leadership by describing the vision that the members should follow. Inspired by the vision, employees will spontaneously collaborate to bring it into being, thereby avoiding the need for planning and authority structures. Welch was clearly transformational, bringing radical change to General Electric, and he is also an able and articulate leader. But Tichy himself describes how Welch gained a clear vision of what the company should be only *after* much of the transformation had been accomplished. As shown in Figure 5.1, many different versions of the vision were promulgated starting in 1980, when Welch took over, and the emphasis changed as business priorities shifted. There was no clear vision to guide the transformation or in-

spire the troops to spontaneous cooperation without the visible
hand of management.

Many of the early actions taken by Welch were pragmatic
steps to improve company well-being and finances. They were
based on the application of conventional business ideas about
the need for productivity improvement and high market share,
implemented through case by case analysis of each business.
These initiatives required detailed knowledge of the businesses
throughout the management structure: a far cry from leadership by vision. The General Electric case provides little evidence of the central role of a vision around which the clan ral-
lied. Instead, it shows how the rhetoric of the vision helped
make the hierarchy's normal business decisions and operations function in a more acceptable way.

FIGURE 5.1
THE EVOLVING VISION AT GENERAL ELECTRIC

Year	Elements of the Vision
1980	Be number 1 or 2 in your market, or we will fix/close/sell.
1981	Downsize, delayer, be lean and agile.
1982	Quantum change, not incremental change, is needed.
1983	Reality and candor are essential: see the world as it is, not as we would like it to be.
1985	Exist via integrated diversity, not as a conglomerate; be big and small at the same time.
1986	Tune the human engine: release emotional energy by encouraging self-confidence, simplicity, and speed. Accept shared values.
1988	The organization should be boundaryless.
1989	Implement a workout model, a process for continuous improvement and full-scale employee involvement.
1990	Strive for best practice, eliminate "not invented here."
1991	The community should be boundaryless.
1992/93	Emphasize speed and quick market intelligence.

Source: Extracted from Noel M. Tichy and Stratford Sherman, *Control Your Destiny or
Someone Else Will: Lessons in Mastering Change—from the Principles Jack Welch is Using
to Revolutionize GE* (New York: HarperCollins, 1994).

LIMITS OF CLAN CULTURE

Managers like Jack Welch don't substitute a strong clan culture for traditional management, because of the fundamental limitations of clan ideas, particularly in large complex organizations. Studies show that organizations in all industries and countries become more structurally complex as they grow in size. More elaborate structures are necessary as the number of employees to guide and coordinate grows. Critics of formal structure advocate lean, minimalist structures. However, there is no evidence that less elaborate structures are more effective for large organizations. Researchers such as John Child of Cambridge University have concluded that more elaborately structured large organizations actually perform better than large organizations that have somewhat less complex structures.[5] His study of German industry, conducted with Alfred Kieser of Mannheim University, also shows the rise of structural complexity as organizations grow in size.[6] Large organizations necessarily separate their employees into different divisions, business units, departments, sections, and jobs so that each performs distinct work. This formal structure is a far cry from the clan.

Separating the jobs of employees creates not a corporate culture but a series of distinct subcultures. In a large organization, each division will tend to develop its own culture. Within the division, each department may have a distinct culture. The differences in the work performed by each department and in the type of people each hires mean that people in one department think differently from people in the next department. Cultural differences exist between both functions, such as R&D and production, and different business units, such as the locomotive business and the TV business at General Electric. These differences, however, are a source of strength and innovation for the organization as a whole.

Functional Differences

Sharp differences in thinking, culture, and approach within a firm are necessary and desirable, as can be seen by comparing the R&D and manufacturing functions in a typical large company. The goal of the R&D department is to produce innovations. It employs scientists and engineers who work on projects that might last a couple of years. Not until a year or more has gone by will the R&D staff know whether their bright idea works or not. Because these employees are seeking original solutions to novel problems, the organization cannot guide them in their work. It relies on the professional knowledge and talent of the scientists to figure out for themselves what approach to take. R&D employees thus enjoy considerable autonomy. They come and go at odd hours, with their best work sometimes done at home or over the weekend. There is often a laissez-faire or easygoing atmosphere in R&D departments to avoid inhibiting creativity.

In contrast, the goal of the manufacturing department is to produce quality output at low cost. It faces a far more tangible task: to produce products for which the specifications have been defined on machines with known characteristics. There is more stability, too, in that the department may have been making the same product on those machines for a long time. This means that the work can be more tightly circumscribed by schedules, processes, and—dare we suggest it?—work study. Jobs are quite closely defined, through written job definitions and the like. There is immediacy in the manufacturing department, with managers focused on keeping the line flowing and attaining the production target for the day or shift. There is a strictness about adhering to costs, procedures, quality standards, and so on. Employees who are late will typically be punished by reprimand, forfeited pay, or even dismissal. Compared to the R&D department, the manufacturing department has more structured jobs, more punishment, and shorter timeframes. (Many service companies such as McDonald's are governed by similar standards.)

Hence the two departments differ in their goals, timeframes, degree of structure, and strictness. The research of Paul Lawrence and Jay Lorsch of the Harvard Business School has shown that high-performing organizations have large differences between their functional departments with respect to these factors.[7] To a person going from one department to another, it might seem like two different worlds.

A manager imbued with the theory of corporate culture would seek to reduce the differences between the manufacturing and R&D departments. He or she would seek to create homogeneity, despite inevitable resistance by workers and reduced effectiveness. An R&D department run on stricter lines will become less creative as conformity becomes the new norm. Likewise, a manufacturing department run in a more laissez-faire fashion will lose its discipline, so that deadlines will be missed, variations will destroy quality, costs will increase, and output will decline.

Differences Among Businesses

Large organizations handle more than functional complexity. They are also often involved in a range of different businesses, seeking to gain benefits through synergies or interrelationships. Thus, General Electric not only invents and builds major industrial equipment and components such as generators, locomotives, and auto parts. It also has enormous financing businesses, including insurance, brokering, and investment banking, that were initially based on financing equipment sales but quickly took on a life of their own. Even within manufacturing at General Electric, differences between businesses are marked. Auto parts are made to set designs, delivered on a just-in-time basis, and involve repetitive processes that need to be continually improved. Power generation plants require far more design for each unit, delivery timeframes run to years and even decades, and fundamental engineering breakthroughs can provide an edge. If there is to be a guiding corporate culture, it had better be able to tolerate both extremes, or performance will suffer. Hence, the "rules of the clan" in firms like General Electric are inevitably very general: "Strive for leadership," "Be cooperative," or "Follow high standards."

These are hardly prescriptions that will replace the need for management. At most, they are outlines of a broad pathway.

When the culture and clan from one business unit are thoughtlessly imposed on others with different requirements, the results can be disastrous. The debacles of many investment banks in the late 1980s and more recently illustrate the point. Within investment banks there are typically two kinds of business. The first provides advice and funding to large corporations and governments; for example, it might advise a corporation on the need for and raising of equity or debt capital. The second type includes the traders who deal in huge sums in the money, bond, and derivatives markets—the screen jockeys, rocket scientists, and players. Most banks are involved in both types of business but recognize and respect the sharp differences in culture. When one culture dominates, there is usually trouble in store. For example, when the traders run rife and impose their culture of the jungle on the firm, prudential practices become sloppy and huge losses occur. Similarly, if advisers try to impose their caution and risk profile on traders, business can dry up. Successful banks like Goldman Sachs manage both types of culture within a framework of general values such as integrity and cooperation across the firm. Banks plagued with problems such as Salomon Brothers in its bond trading of the late 1980s, vividly described by Michael Lewis in *Liar's Poker*,[8] let the trading culture dominate to the point where analysis and care were reviled and macho behavior placed on a pedestal.

Research shows that companies with strong corporate cultures, that is to say, those that are homogeneous across their constituent departments, are low performers in the long run.[9] Such strong corporate culture companies are high performers for a while, as their shared norms make cooperation easier. However, cooperation through sameness destroys the creative tension between departments that gives rise to innovation and creates undue risk aversion via excessive checks and balances. Joanne Martin of Stanford University has warned of the dangers of shaping corporate culture into a unifying consensus that can leave the organization stuck in the status quo, unable to make needed changes.[10]

The recipe for effective organization is not homogenization. Rather, effective organizations foster distinct subcultures so that differences are respected and can flourish. They foster communication and collaboration among subcultures so that the differences between them remain intact. Employees collaborate at the points where subcultures touch, such as new product innovation projects or joint sales from different businesses, but otherwise work independently within their own subcultures.

Arranging, comprehending, and coordinating these subcultures is a significant challenge and is the role of managers. The managers run each unit. Higher-level managers orchestrate a group of businesses and departments. Paul Lawrence and Jay Lorsch showed that in successful companies with high innovation, significant numbers of additional managers had to be appointed to handle collaboration between departments.

Hence, successful corporations—especially if innovative, large, and diverse—have anything but a unified corporate culture. Attempts to impose a unifying culture other than at the most general level would be counterproductive. Such attempts would stifle creativity and innovation by suppressing differences in thinking that reflect real differences in goals, technologies, products, and customers among the various parts of the same company. And the monoculture would increase risks, as the experience of Wall Street firms shows.

Customers and the Clan

The boundaryless organization means there are neither internal walls nor walls separating the corporation from its customers and suppliers, who become clan members or at least clan cousins. In some models, the conventional organization dissolves altogether. The organization becomes a network, a web of relationships with customers and suppliers in which the boundaries of the old corporation disappear. The merging of the organization with its customers and suppliers is to be accomplished through electronic hookups that pass information instantaneously across the erstwhile boundary. Nike's "production expatriates" (people employed by Nike who live near and work at its suppliers) and Wal-Mart's electronic links to suppliers (which generate orders as sales are recorded at the stores' checkouts) are recent examples.

There is merit to the principle that corporations should cooperate closely with customers to better meet their needs. This, in turn, can be furthered by working closely with suppliers in order to quickly and cheaply procure quality inputs. Electronic information exchange can assist. But none of this means the end of the corporation or of boundaries between corporations. To talk of the "network organization" sounds as if it is a replacement for existing organizational structures, such as the divisional design. There is no evidence that this is happening. The corporation retains its core internal structure and builds communications lines to connect with customers and suppliers. There is no indication that the corporation abandons its internal structure, though it may alter it.

Nor is there any reason to expect that network developments will lead to the abandonment of internal structures and the dissolution of the corporation. There is nothing new in networking across organizational boundaries. In the furniture quarter of eighteenth-century Paris, individual firms would contract out processes such as gilding, and this involved the sharing of plans. On occasion, materials, apprentices, and so on would be shared, moving fluidly back and forth among firms. This fluidity at the boundaries of firms did not mean that the individual firms dissolved into one large firm. The modern furniture industry retains distinct firms to this day. Likewise, the eighteenth-century furniture firms did not merge with their wealthy patrons to become workshops in the manor houses of the aristocracy.

The present-day electronic sharing of blueprints and information among the corporation, its clients, and its suppliers differs from these earlier network transactions only in degree.

Modern corporations are larger and move much more information internally than the earlier firms, so some external quantitative increase is to be expected. It does not signify the end of the corporation as we know it.

Moreover, there can be internal movement across boundaries without those boundaries dissolving. Millions of people enter and leave the United States each year. This does not mean that the U.S. government has ceased to exist, or that American and Mexican policies are one. Organizations may transact business with each other yet retain a sense of their own identity and distinct self-interest. For commercial organizations, it is precisely pursuit of self-interest that has led them to transact with other organizations in the first place. To attain the maximum gain from these transactions there is much to be said for a high degree of collaboration, with sharing and blending. Yet there are some secrets that the corporation will not wish to disclose to partners, such as proprietary products and processes that provide a competitive advantage. And there will be times when even the closest partners will have different interests.

Thus, successful corporations are maintaining their boundaries and will continue to do so. They will draw a distinction between insiders and outsiders and will treat people accordingly. To say that the organization should aim to be boundaryless in its relationship with customers is high-flown rhetoric that declares an ambition for a close relationship. Such statements may be useful, especially when the practical limitations of that ambition are understood. Only a fool takes rhetoric literally.

The danger is that when rhetoric enters the floating world of management theory it takes on a life of its own. The idea of the boundaryless organization is advocated in the quite literal sense of organizations becoming one with their customers. And this dogma is backed by the authority of Jack Welch and the success of General Electric. Yet, to say that General Electric is boundaryless is to assert that General Electric has dissolved and become indistinguishable from its customers. This has not happened. Shareholders in General Electric still hold the

shares only of General Electric and not of its customers—
though General Electric's share price is clearly affected by the
relationship with its customers and their fortunes.

CLANS AND INDIVIDUAL DIVERSITY

Clans comprise similar people who know each other for a long
time, even for life, so they are socially homogeneous rather
than diverse. Perhaps the nearest thing to clans among work
organizations in the West are communes. Here, people are
united by values that govern how they work and play together.
There is a strong sense of common purpose and fate. The
norms are usually egalitarian with hierarchy and status differences condemned. A major sociological investigation of communes in America concluded that a core feature was lack of diversity, in that they were composed of people who were fairly
similar.[11] This is echoed in elite organizations such as the officer corps of the British Army or the trading team at Salomon
Brothers in the late 1980s. These organizations have clan-like
memberships strongly committed to the organization and its
culture. Recruits are drawn from a narrow range: British public school boys or aggressive MBAs with particular ambition.
Thus, there is a similarity of outlook and shared values on
which these organizations can build.

Ouchi, the theorist of clan organization, candidly admits
that clans not only lack diversity but can be sexist and racist:

> With respect to sex and race, Type Z companies have a tendency
> to be sexist and racist. This is another paradox, because while
> Type Z companies typically work much harder and care much
> more about offering equality of opportunities to minorities, in
> some ways they have much greater obstacles to overcome than
> do Type A companies. As I visited the managers in the high-tech-
> nology Type A, I was struck by the ethnic diversity among the
> upper levels of management: Spanish-Americans, Asian-Ameri-
> cans, Hungarian-Americans, and Anglo-Saxon-Americans. At
> company A, new promotion opportunity is simply awarded to

that candidate who has the best "bottom-line" for the past few periods . . . The only thing that counts is the bottom line, and thus a diverse group of people make it to the top . . .

At company Z the cast of top managers is so homogeneous that one member of my research team characterized the dominant culture as "Boy Scout Macho". That is, the top management is wholesome, disciplined, hard-working, and honest, but unremittingly white, male, and middle class.[12]

Thus, the shared goals and intimacy are based upon homogeneity at the sacrifice of diversity. The Japanese corporation on which the Type Z is modeled is even less tolerant of diversity, as Ouchi candidly admits: "Probably no form of organization is more sexist or racist than the Japanese corporation."[13]

Yet an important feature of work organizations in many countries is increasing diversity. Unlike Japan, with its strong cultural and racial homogeneity, nations like the United States, Canada, Australia, and many parts of Europe include people of diverse backgrounds. Organizations are now employing people from a wider range of racial and ethnic backgrounds, and women are increasingly part of the paid work force. The internationalization of large firms adds to this trend. Increasing diversity is also occurring at more senior managerial levels. The broader range of beliefs, values, and expectations is seen as beneficial in dealing with an increasingly diverse set of customers, as changing demographics make societies themselves more diverse. Moreover, by drawing on a larger pool of people, beyond just white males, organizations can increase the number of highly qualified people in their ranks, for there are many women and nonwhites of high ability who were previously excluded from our corporations. Thus, it becomes less feasible and less desirable to try to turn our organizations into clans of homogeneous people who think alike. The trend is going the other way.

Diversity promotes more reliance on formal organization. In many large organizations, diversity is increasing through policies that ensure equal employment opportunity. No longer can jobs be filled via the old-boy network. Instead, vacancies are advertised in the mass media and we see the use of objective criteria such as educational qualifications and culture-free ability tests. Informal clan-type employment approaches are being replaced by more formal, objective—dare we say bureaucratic—employment approaches in order to increase and deal with employee diversity.

Once employed, the more diverse mix of people requires different management. In the old clan-type organizations, new recruits would already know about the organization and its work and would be imbued with similar values. The more diverse work force knows less of the organization and reflects a wide range of values. Elaborate orientation and training programs conducted by specialists become more common—McDonald University, General Electric's Crotonville, and Motorola University are just a few examples. There is less reliance on informal communications because employees may huddle with their own groups and be cut off from information from outside. Videos, newsletters, mass meetings, and formal declarations down the chain of command supplement the grapevine.

With less solidarity and fellow feeling, more effort is needed to build trust. A grievance procedure may be set up to deal with allegations of discrimination or sexual harassment. Meetings between manager and subordinates on personnel issues are documented. While such formality may be considered tedious, it is an inevitable consequence of the move toward a more diverse work force, and the exact opposite of clan management.

Clans are really the old style of informal management, which today would seem patriarchal and ethnocentric. Clan management is incompatible with the aspiration for, and movement toward, a more diverse work force. For clans to work, the work force would need to return to being a homogeneous gathering of, for example, white males of Anglo-Saxon Protestant background. This is not going to happen. The clock will not run backwards. It is counter to the legitimate aspirations of too many of the people who now compose our work forces. It is socially and politically infeasible.

Work force diversity does create a need to articulate and imbue people with some unifying ideas and values that help the organization function. But we reiterate that these, while important, are not a substitute for structure, process, and detailed, firm-specific analysis and action.

THE DARKER SIDE

The interpretation of General Electric that Tichy and Sherman offer their readers is quite exotic. They liken Welch to a revolutionary political leader who transforms society. This is achieved through vision, iconoclasm, and empowerment of the masses. But it is achieved also through the use of power. Tichy and Sherman refer to control of the police, schools, and media as the means by which the elite drives the masses. According to their account at General Electric, the police included the internal auditors and others involved in budgetary controls, the schools are the training programs and institutes—most notably Crotonville—and the media includes all communication with employees and people outside the company.[14] Such images give managerial decisions color and drama—more interesting than just divesting the TV or appliance businesses. But they also point up the use of coercive power by the hierarchy at General Electric to force change upon the organization. They are images of force, rather than of persuasion through reasoned discussion between equals.

In theory, the clan model works through shared thinking, so force is unnecessary. However, the idea of the transformational leader who inspires the clan's members has been grafted on. This is Moses, down from the mountaintop, rallying the children of Israel with the tablets of stone. Later, this transformational leader is accorded power in the political realm, like Lenin, whom Tichy and Sherman parallel to Welch.[15]

Why have clans led to coercive power? The answer is that the clan is such an unnatural thing in modern societies that efforts to produce clans encounter great resistance. Thus, recourse is made to force. Hitler was trying to impose an Aryan national so-cialist clan onto the complex, pluralistic societies of Germany and the nations to the east. Freethinking intellectuals, Jews, Polish academics, and Slav nationalists were impediments to the new order and had to be eliminated, in his view. Similarly, Lenin and Stalin were trying to impose a communist, classless, internation-alist clan onto the Russian people, despite their centuries of reli-gious belief and loyalty to the Tsar. The royalists, intellectuals, re-ligious leaders, and independent farmers were impediments to communism and had to be crushed, according to Stalin.

The beguiling model of the clan leads to extreme actions by leaders possessed of the necessary power, because their goal is not in accord with reality. Of course, the leaders of our corpora-tions will not take such violent coercive action. They will not have the desire or the means. But we should not be surprised if theo-rists such as Tichy and Sherman embrace more coercive images of change, for this is where the crusade for the clan leads.

As coercion takes hold, people in the organization suppress or suspend independent thought and action. What isn't in line with the clan rhetoric cannot be contemplated. As long as the established rhetoric fits the needs of customers, success rein-forces the strength of the clan's approach. But when danger signs appear on the horizon, no one speaks up. For years, IBM was cited as an exemplar of good management via strong cul-ture. But when the market changed, fragmenting into myriad segments, and customers wanted open architecture, unbun-dled services, and competitive prices, IBM either could not hear or would not listen. The only signal the culture would let in was "We need to do much better (but not be fundamentally different)." Even an outside CEO is battling to disestablish the entrenched beliefs and approaches. IBM's too strong corporate culture was imposed by the iron will of its founder, Thomas J. Watson, and his biographer likens him to Stalin.[16]

In every strong, coercive clan are sown the seeds of its own destruction.

CONCLUSION

The notion of clans and culture does not offer an alternative way to manage firms. Large complex organizations need to function through the clear assignment of responsibilities. A hard-nosed, results-based orientation lies behind professed soft-focus harmony, as is clear from closer examination of leading firms in Japan and the West. Moreover, the clan and culture fads can, if taken to extremes, be harmful. Diversity is essential for business survival; it allows the corporation to tap into a larger pool of highly qualified people whose diverse backgrounds match today's customers. The attempt to create a corporate clan of people who are all similar, in order to manage without hierarchy, would lead to homogeneity and thus frustrate the aspiration toward diversity. Those who cannot hear the changing drumbeat cannot dance to the new rhythm. And diversity is demanded in modern, mobile societies where firms no longer comprise a single type of individual in terms of gender, race, nationality, class, and education.

Successful organizations are composed of different task groups, such as functions and divisions, that have their own cultures. Thus, the organization is composed of numerous distinct subcultures, each attuned to its own role, such as manufacturing or research. Good management fosters such differences and then coordinates them through project teams, matrix structures, and similar formal devices. This may be undergirded by a common corporate culture shared by all employees, for example, a commitment to customer service, but agreement on some things should not stifle disagreement on other things, for that is where the dynamic tension so necessary for adaptive change comes from. Moreover, employees, in their similarities and differences, are still all guided by a hierarchy of managers. This is a proven part of the success of large corporations and the idea of replacing it all by a clan in which consensus replaces hierarchy is an attractive but false trail.

6

THE BOARD OF DIRECTORS
AS WATCHDOG

The first four false trails are ways in which managers are urged to improve what they do inside the organization—flattening structure, acting before analyzing, using techniques, and creating a clan-like culture. The fifth trail is different. It offers the false prospect of success by ensuring that management is kept firmly in check under the watchful eyes of a vigilant, independent board of directors. The majority of these directors, and in particular the chair, should be part-time nonexecutives, spending an average two days per month on the company's affairs.

The fifth trail appeals to those who see the solution to all organizational problems in terms of "fixing things at the top." Make the board more activist, more independent, a stronger critic and scrutineer, appoint independent, strong-minded people to safeguard the interests of shareholders. Then have the board be tough on poor performance in the interests of shareholders—monitor relentlessly, KATN (kick ass, take names), fire nonperformers. With this kind of board, there is no place for incompetent managers to hide.

Activist boards have forced out chief executives at General Motors, IBM, and American Express in the United States, at Littlewoods in Britain, and at the Westpac Banking Corporation in Australia. The coup is generally swift, pursuing a set piece along the following lines.

The first rumblings occur when the board discusses, usually in gentle terms, the fact that performance has not been quite up to investor expectations for a number of years. Recognizing that something needs to be done, management then sets in motion an improvement program. If such a program is already in place, the talk switches to "accelerating progress" or "more decisive actions." While action by the CEO and his or her team may be vigorous, results rarely emerge quickly enough to satisfy the real-time demands of investors, the financial press, and a board under fire. Board members begin to talk outside the meetings about "the lack of progress," with no consideration of the time required to turn a corporation around. A large institutional investor may have a quiet chat with influential directors. The press is usually less reticent: "CEO should go," "Results Continue to Disappoint under Current Leadership," "The Problem is in the Executive Suite."

The outside directors then meet privately without the CEO or any other executives present or even aware of the meeting. "We need to act. . . . What can we do? . . . We must change the CEO." Lawyers are called in, a termination package is prepared, a successor—often from within—is spoken to in confidence. A few of the board members then meet with the CEO. "You no longer enjoy the confidence of the Board. . . . Accept this package with grace immediately or we will not be so generous." From rooster to feather duster in less than an hour!

Like many of the other false trails, this one, too, has some attractive aspects. Especially during the 1980s, when takeovers, restructuring, and management buyouts reached a peak, the boards of many firms were seen to be doing a poor job. Everyone knows that some boards failed; they were conned or corrupted by unscrupulous managers who were aided and abetted by greedy bankers. Books based on actual accounts tell the story: *Den of Thieves, Barbarians at the Gate, The Predators' Ball, Maxwell.* Others then build on the stories to argue forcefully for more power in the hands of outsiders. A stock market crash such as occurred in 1987 underscores the impression of board failure.

For example, *Power and Accountability*, written by commentators Robert Monks and Nell Minow after the "excesses of the 1980s" and taking the view of the professional investor managing other people's money, argues that corporate accountability to shareholders is a myth, and that boards and institutional investors must reassert their control over management to protect not only profitability but even "the quality of the air we breathe . . . the water we drink, even where we live."[1] "A provocative answer to anyone alarmed by *Barbarians at the Gate*," shouts the book's jacket cover.

The new order calls for an all-powerful board that keeps the power and authority of managers firmly in check. Managers become hired hands, subject to being fired on a moment's notice. Boards themselves ought to fall on their swords if performance declines. Takeovers should be encouraged to keep everyone on their toes.

The ideas are now accepted doctrine. In the United States, there are widespread calls to move to a board model with an outside chair and to take steps to ensure that control of the board is in the hands of independent part-time directors. In the United Kingdom, the respected Cadbury Committee[2] made similar proposals. Parallel moves are afoot in Canada and Australia. Stock markets seek to put requirements for board composition into the rules that listed firms must observe if their shares are to be publicly traded. Increasingly onerous regulation of corporations covering accounting, disclosure, and capital structure is also appearing. The faddish concern with the need for outside control of managers by boards of directors seems unassailable.

However, other than well-told stories such as *Barbarians at the Gate*, the evidence in support of this trail is extremely weak. In other areas of public policy, no one would argue that a few unofficial pieces of "investigative reporting" ought to provide the basis for major initiatives with respect to regulation of large firms and the environment in which they operate. Criminal law isn't rewritten because of a popular book on O.J. Simpson or the

Manson case. Yet, despite the importance to society of the large management-intensive firm, just such half-baked proposals founded on a few exceptional cases of misdeed are the basis for a redesign of the entire board and governance system, despite most managers and directors being well-meaning and honest.

In this chapter, we argue that the ideas behind the fifth trail are potentially as damaging to corporations as the other false trails. We shall offer as evidence the large-scale studies that demonstrate that independent boards fail to improve corporate performance. Rather, the studies caution against foisting these medicines on the corporate sector—in short, yet another false trail. We begin by chronicling the rise of professional managers and their subsequent fall from grace, for this is the basis of the fifth false trail: the board as watchdog over management.

THE RISE OF THE MANAGER

Traditionally, businesses were run by their owners under a system called proprietorial capitalism. This worked while each business was small. As populations increased and as modern transportation and technologies developed, the scale of businesses grew. Businesses soon needed finances beyond what the owner-manager could supply. Hence the creation of the modern, large corporation in which outsiders held stock or shares in the company but did not manage it. In the twentieth century, it became common for large corporations to be run by professional managers who were not part of the founding family and who might own little or none of the corporation. Thus, ownership became split from management, a development hailed even in the 1930s as "the managerial revolution." The new form of management was called managerial capitalism.

The managerial revolution was accompanied by worries that the outside owner would be defrauded by the managers now in control of the company. The board of directors was seen as a check on these managers, ensuring that they took care of the interests of the outside owners rather than favoring their own interests. The legal doctrine held that the board of directors had a "fiduciary duty" to protect the interests of shareholders. In the traditional firm, then, the board was literally supposed to direct the firm. The directors would often include persons of wealth, privilege, and high social standing. They sat over the managers, who were mere "company servants." Managers, while running the company day to day, had no specific right to be on the board. They might sit outside its door and be summoned to give an account of themselves or not, as the directors saw fit. Elements of this ethos have survived in Britain, where managers are still sometimes said to be company servants.

Of course, in reality, because the managers ran the company, they had to be included in board discussions for them to be at all meaningful. Attendance by the CEO and chief financial manager was common, though they were not always accorded the status of board directors. Over time, professional managers, the CEO and heads of key functions such as finance or operations, were admitted to the board as directors. In some companies, much was made of the fact that, as directors, these managers were required to throw off their narrow functional perspectives and view the company as a whole, as befitted a director.

With the growth and success of the modern large enterprise, the status of the professional manager also increased. The burgeoning complexity of the corporation made the input of professional managers at board meetings even more necessary. Thus, managers began to sit on boards in greater numbers, making up more of the directorships. Traditionally, to provide an impartial check on the managers, who were also directors, the chairman of the board (invariably male) was an outsider. However, in some large corporations, the top manager—the CEO or president—was made chairman of the board. Thus, the same person was simultaneously chairman and CEO. Hence, the professional manager was now heading the board. This practice was most widespread in America. At one time, about three out of every four corporate boards were chaired by the company's CEO. This was a high-water mark in the ascendancy of the professional manager, giving him unprecedented status and authority in the corporation.

To some commentators, CEO chairmanships compromised the independence of corporate boards. They were seen as neutering the boards by leaving managers free to indulge their self-interest at the expense of the shareholders. In England, this American practice was described as "chaps marking their own exam papers" and "poachers turned gamekeepers." The English retained the tradition of the chairman who was independent of management, and certainly not managing director (i.e., CEO).

In the large American corporation, the CEO as chair was balanced to some extent by the fact that most of the directors—about two out of three—were outsiders who were not managers. However, some studies estimate that in practice, about half of these outside directors were not really independent of management, being retired managers of the company, relatives of management, or suppliers, contractors, or consultants to management.[3] These "gray directors" were seen to owe some allegiance to management and therefore to share the interests of the managers rather than of the outside owners. Similarly, many outside directors had little equity in the corporation, making their representation of outside owners tenuous.[4] Outside directors were often selected by the CEO and were beholden to him for their position, pay, and perquisites. Most studies of boards in the 1970s found them to be toothless tigers.[5] One key study found that boards did not proactively make decisions but rather reacted to the proposals of the managers.[6] A Harvard Business School study of the early 1970s reported that outside directors did not ask discerning questions, lacked information about the company, and were dependent upon management for such information.[7] Yet, in the public mind, boards continued to be "sounding boards" and the outside directors were depicted as wise individuals who asked penetrating questions.

In reality, the board of directors was generally passive, reviewing what the managers did and not intervening in the company unless there was a crisis. Only if the managers seemed to be failing in their duties, reflected in consistently poor returns to share-holders or breakdowns in legality or ethics, did the board step in to remove and replace senior managers. The board was a fail-safe device actuated only when management seriously malfunc-tioned. In the expanding Western economies typical of the 1950s and 1960s, there were few profit crises, and public concern about corporate ethics was less than today. Thus, boards could remain passive, leaving professional managers to run things.

The system of managerial capitalism worked. Professional managers were hailed as a new force for socially useful produc-tion and prosperity. They were vaunted as twentieth-century professionals. Professional managers were skilled at running the complex modern corporation. In fact, they were considered so skilled and talented that they could run anything more effec-tively than anyone else. They could move out from their existing base business and run widely differing businesses, from steel to insurance. With professional managers at their helm, corpora-tions diversified to become conglomerates. The stock market loved these high-growth conglomerates and investors paid a premium for the privilege of owning their stock.

Managerial capitalism reached a high point during the 1960s, with America at the apex of the system. With its large, di-versified corporations run by hierarchies of managers in com-plex divisionalized structures, America was a role model emu-lated by the rest of world. Management consulting firms such as McKinsey carried this message around the globe.

THE FALL FROM GRACE

Even at the high point, there were rumblings against the triumph of the professional managers. Thoughtful commentators pointed out that boards of directors were not working as they were sup-posed to and were not full-blooded watchdogs over managers.

By the 1970s and 1980s, many large corporations attracted public attention for failing in their purposes. International com-petition increased and the products of major U.S. and European manufacturers seemed shoddy by comparison. The perception of poor quality and dated designs, such as gas-guzzling automobiles, dented the reputation of major corporations and their managers. Stories began to appear, like John DeLorean's revelations of senior executives snoozing during meetings at GM headquarters. Ethical scandals attracted media attention, such as bribery allegations against Lockheed in its bid for Japanese orders. Performance problems leading to the loss of profitability and market share of large corporations engendered a feeling of financial crisis. Management came to be seen as overpaying itself with huge remuneration and benefit packages, and as indulging its interests via expensive diversifications that seemed to benefit sellers rather than acquirers. These perceived failures in management led to the question, What is the board doing?

Large corporations became subject to hostile takeovers justified by the failure of managers to deliver wealth to shareholders. The acquirer would supply new, fitter managers who would more assiduously serve the shareholders. Target corporations mustered defenses such as paying off corporate raiders with greenmail or installing poison pills. Managers fearing ouster guaranteed themselves large termination payouts through golden parachutes. Boards played a central role in responding to takeovers. Thus, by the 1980s, the board of directors was center stage.

The crash of 1987, the ensuing scandals at savings and loans institutions, and such phenomena as highly leveraged companies, junk bonds, and plain fraud were catalysts for more strident and serious calls for reform.

A key proposal called for ensuring the independence of boards of directors by having the chair be an outsider rather than the CEO. A related proposal called for a majority of the board to be outsiders independent of management. Directors should hold substantial numbers of shares so that they would have the shareholders' interests at heart. Boards were to be given better and more detailed information in order to monitor managers more closely. Boards should also be actively involved in shaping corporate strategy rather than merely responding to plans proposed by the managers. Boards were no longer to rubber-stamp decisions in a display of conformance to externally mandated regulations; they were to drive the performance of the corporation.

Above all, boards must control managers and replace them when they failed to deliver high financial performance. Boards should plot key profit and shareholder return figures for the corporation over time and compare them with the averages for the industry and the market. Where the numbers drop below average for some years, managers are to be called to account in no uncertain terms. Thus board members, as representatives of the owners, are to be more truly directors. Where boards do not carry out their role effectively, the large institutional investors should move in and install new directors to take charge. The sovereign power of the owners is being asserted over that of managers, who are to be reduced to their supposedly rightful place as company servants.

This change in the perceived role of the board represents the resurgence of proprietorial capitalism and the decline of managerial capitalism. Owners are again to play the lead role in managing their corporations. It is the second coming of proprietorial power.

Proprietorship is reintroduced also through the provision of incentives to senior managers. In order to align their interests with those of outside shareholders, some part of managerial compensation is to take the form of shares—by means of share option schemes, for example. Likewise, managers are offered bonuses keyed to the returns received by shareholders via share price increases and the like. By accepting some part of their compensation in these forms rather than straight salary, managers accept the same risks as shareholders. Such compensation schemes have been widely adopted in large American corporations to end the conflict of interest between managers and shareholders. There have been suggestions that board directors should themselves be compensated in shares or share options rather than fees to align their personal financial interests with those of outside shareholders.

Owners have also sought a more active role. In particular, institutional investors—mainly pension and insurance funds—

are urged to heed the call of Robert Monks and Nell Minow to be more involved in selecting directors, monitoring the board, and expressing their views informally or by voting.[8] The traditional institutional investor's choices were to remain passive, side with management, or, if too dissatisfied with a corporation, sell out. Now investors are beginning to act more like owners, wanting to be involved in the business.

The constant fear of hostile takeover also disciplines corporate managers to heed the interests of shareholders. The Darwinian rules of business dictate that companies that underperform will (or should) be taken over. The incumbent managers will tend to be apprehensive of their fate at the hands of new owners, especially when they have sought to repulse them and provoked a hostile takeover. This fear of takeover is thought to keep managers industrious in the service of existing shareholders, since the cost of underperforming is loss of their jobs.

The increasing use of leverage by corporations during the 1970s and '80s brought their managers tougher debt discipline. Because free cash flow was preassigned to pay the interest on debt, there was less for managers to play with. The leveraged and management buyouts of the 1980s not only replaced equity with debt, but also replaced professional managers with owner-managers. These included the principals of specialist buyout firms such as KKR. The new breed of activist owner thus provided yet another better alternative to the discredited professional manager. In the management buyout, the professional manager became the owner, thereby reinstating proprietorship. Michael Jensen of the Harvard Business School proclaimed the death of the public corporation.[9] The key was the reduced discretion of professional managers and the greater role of proprietors. Again, managerial capitalism was being overturned in favor of proprietorial capitalism.

In many quarters today, the large corporation run by professional managers is suspect. Its managers are widely distrusted as idle, incompetent, unethical, or clever only in pursuit of their own self-aggrandizement. Strong checks on their power are seen as vital. These are provided most crucially through close control by the board of directors. Manager motivation is sought through financial incentives based on profits and share prices. These are supplemented by the external disciplines of takeover threat, debt, and activist institutional owners. The professional corporate managers sit embattled, encircled by forces that would strip them of their powers.

These contemporary movements have deep roots in popular sentiment, and are reinforced by seemingly authoritative pronouncements. However, they are founded upon sand. Many of the undergirding beliefs are wrong or substantially in error. We will now rebut them one by one, and we will make the case for empowering rather than hobbling professional managers.

THE MYTH OF THE "MANAGERIAL REVOLUTION"

The concern that professional managers in large corporations are acting against the interests of outside owners goes back to the classic book by Adolf Berle and Gardiner Means first published in 1932, *The Modern Corporation and Private Property*.[10] This is repeatedly used by contemporary writers as the basis for understanding the managerial revolution. Berle and Means argued that corporations controlled by managers, rather than by owners, consume more value in managerial benefits and so return less value to owners. However, the research methods used by Berle and Means to back up their claims were primitive by modern standards and so limit the credibility of their findings. Moreover, when the issue was reexamined 50 years later by George Stigler of the University of Chicago, a Nobel laureate in economics, the weaknesses in Berle and Means' ideas became clearer. Together with a colleague, Claire Friedland, Stigler analyzed large U.S. corporations during the period when Berle and Means worked. They found no evidence that the managerially controlled companies paid their managers more than owner-controlled corporations, or that managerially controlled corporations produced less profit from their assets. Stigler and Friedland concluded:

Our own statistical analyses, using only data and methods familiar to economists of the time, yield no clear evidence that the
management-dominated corporations differed much from
owner-dominated companies in practices of executive compensation or in the utilization of assets to produce profits.[11]

This calls into question the Berle and Means theory and the
spectre of the Managerial Revolution. Further, there is no factual
basis for believing that there is a widespread problem of managers of large corporations feathering their own nests at the expense of shareholders. There are instances of individual corporations in which managers take advantage of outside shareholders
and other financiers. However, there is no automatic tendency
for this to happen just because a firm has grown large and the
owners have passed control over to professional managers.

The economist John Galbraith, who has studied several eras in
which corporate collapses have occurred, offers a different explanation of why society seems to turn on or tighten control of management from time to time. In a recent book, Galbraith notes that
market crashes such as the one experienced in 1987 have been re-
peated many times over hundreds of years. Some notable crashes
include those that followed the frenzy in Holland's tulip market in
the seventeenth century, the South Sea Bubble of the early eigh-
teenth century, and the booms and busts of the 1890s, 1920s,
1930s, and 1960s. There are a number of common elements in
each situation: people mesmerized by the idea of easy money, a
public impression that with money come intelligence and acu-
men, a bidding up of values that confirms these impressions, and,
finally, mass disillusion and crash. In Galbraith's words:

Those who are involved never wish to attribute stupidity to themselves. Markets also are theologically sacrosanct. Some blame can
be placed on the more spectacular or felonious of the previous spec-
ulators, but not on the recently enchanted (and now disenchanted)
participants. The least important questions are the ones most em-
phasized: What triggered the crash? Were there some special factors that made it so dramatic or drastic? Who should be punished?

Yet beyond a better perception of the speculative tendency and process itself, there probably is not a great deal that can be done. Regulation outlawing financial incredulity or mass euphoria is not a practical possibility. If applied generally [to such human condition], the result would be an impressive, perhaps oppressive, and certainly ineffective body of law.[12]

Galbraith's reasoning leads to the conclusion that calls for board independence and control of management are all about finding scapegoats for the poor judgments and decisions of professional and amateur investors during periods of market madness. The reforms have nothing to do with good management and everything to do with the politics of blame.

Let us now turn to the central issue: the board of directors.

THE FALLACY OF INDEPENDENCE

At the heart of the proposals to reshape boards is the idea that the independence of the board members is critical. The real challenge for boards, however, is not independence but performance. People don't invest in companies to participate in a political process or to exercise power. They invest in order to obtain returns, and they expect the companies they invest in to produce better returns than other companies. Can an independent board be more effective at causing managers to earn above-average returns for shareholders? One factor is independence, in the sense of directors being free to make decisions that they believe are in the interests of the firm. But there are other qualities that can help a company, for example, competence, insight, experience, judgment, knowledge, imagination, and political skill. Independence only becomes an issue when the company is faced with managers who are dishonest or untrustworthy. Where managers basically have good motives and are trying hard to improve performance, independence is irrelevant and these other qualities far more important. What research study after research study shows is that board independence seems to have little to do with performance.

Independent Directors and Chair

The first assumption of the independent director dogma is that boards made up predominantly of independent outside directors produce better results than boards made up predominantly of managers. Researchers have examined companies to see whether this is true. The results are fascinating. Most studies fail to find that outsider-dominated boards are associated with more profitable companies. On the contrary, most studies find that outsider-dominated boards produce poorer company performance and that insider-dominated boards are superior.[13] These results are meaningful because most researchers start out expecting to prove that outsider boards are superior. A majority of managers on a board may reduce its independence. However, this is offset by the insider board's far greater expertise in the company's business, leading to higher performance than under the outsider board.

A pioneering researcher was Stanley Vance of the School of Business Administration at the University of Oregon. His initial study revealed the benefits to company performance provided by managers rather than outside directors:

> Inside boards are superior in performance to outsider boards; outside boards with relatively strong management representation are superior to those lacking such management representation; next in sequence of excellence are managements with outsiders who are predominantly "local" businessmen; at the very bottom of the performance "totem pole" are firms with outside boards comprised largely of absentee directors.[14]

A subsequent study by Vance reinforced this finding. High corporate financial performance resulted only from board directors who were also managers of *the same* corporation. Moreover, low corporate financial performance resulted from independent directors who possessed managerial experience *in other industries*. Vance concludes that "bringing in another company's chief executive to sit on the board is no substitute for full-time dedicated company employees."[15] This finding is

important because having a CEO from another company become a director is widely favored today as a way to get independence combined with managerial expertise onto the board;
however, the Vance study suggests that this practice may reduce company performance. Also, company performance was
not affected by the degree of ownership among board members. This stood Vance's initial belief in the value of proprietorship, that is, of owners as directors, on its head. Thus, the
Vance studies challenge conventional wisdom by showing that
the company's own managers, not necessarily independent
outsiders, make the best directors.

Similarly, research by other scholars has failed to consistently
support the idea that an independent outsider chair produces
better performance than a combined CEO/chair. The results of
the studies are mixed, with one supporting the independent chair
but some supporting neither.[16] However, another study supports
the association between the CEO as board chairperson and more
profitable corporations—in contradiction to popular belief.[17] Of
course, with studies finding both for and against the independent
chairperson, the true effect may be nil. One analyst reviewed these
studies and found their average to be essentially zero.[18] Thus,
there may be no superiority to the independent chair.

Even this moderate interpretation means that there is no advantage in having an independent person chairing the board rather
than the CEO. Nor is there harm in the CEO's also being chair of
the board. Even a cursory look at the real world shows that the type
of chair, inside or outside, is irrelevant. Companies such as Wal-
Mart, Microsoft, and Nike have performed superbly, while GM,
IBM, and Amex have at times struggled—yet all had inside chairs.
British Leyland saw its markets disappear under an outside chair,
while an outside chair presided over the re-invigoration of ICI.

Fortune magazine ran a December 1995 cover story featuring
Coca-Cola and GE as the two companies that ranked top on creating value for their investors. These results were achieved by
men who held the joint role of CEO and chair. Moreover, both
Roberto Goizueta and Jack Welch were appointed CEO-chair in

the spring of 1981, so they have been playing the dual role for over fourteen years. During this time the Market Value Added of Coca-Cola soared by about $55 billion. Having the CEO as board chair did not harm business at Coca-Cola and GE, and allowed them to become the greatest wealth generators for investors.

Thus, with respect to both aspects of the independence of boards of directors—domination by outsiders as directors and chair—the weight of evidence fails to support the idea that independent is better. Managers who are not under the control of outsiders look after their shareholders about as well as those who are so controlled. The widely presumed incompetence and deviousness of professional managers is a false generalization.

There are several ways in which manager-controlled corporations are supposed to fritter away corporate performance unless checked by a powerful board of independent outsiders. Diversification is one way and underinvestment in technological innovation is another. We will examine each in turn.

The Independent Board and Diversification

Corporate diversification away from the core is seen as a poor strategy. There is currently a widespread belief that it is preferable to "stick to the knitting." Corporations that diversify are seen as harming their shareholders. Given the supposed folly of diversification, the continuing spate of diversifications is explained as managers maximizing their own self-interest at the expense of the outside owners. The managers value the size and growth that diversification brings because their pay and status are based on the number of workers they employ.

In addition, diversification into several unrelated areas offsets decline in any one area, producing more stable corporate performance. With less risk of poor performance, the top managers are more secure in their jobs. In contrast, the outside owners would prefer the corporation to take risks, since risk yields profits. The outside owners hold a portfolio of investments across corporations and this lowers their overall risk.

Hence, by diversifying the corporation the managers take on less risk than the owners would wish. The owners would prefer to hold a portfolio of shares across numerous risk-taking, focused firms. Corporate diversification is thus counterproductive for owners but rational for managers. The existence of diversifying firms is seen as proof that managers are putting their own interests ahead of their shareholders'.

Given the belief that diversification is bad, it seems obvious that the board of directors would want to prevent it by vetoing managerial proposals for acquisitions outside the core competence of the corporation. Thus, a board of directors that is independent of management should allow less diversification. In contrast, a corporation whose board is dominated by managers would diversify more, as the managers pursued their personal goals at the expense of shareholders.

Two studies seeking to prove that insider boards lead to more diversification by their corporations found the opposite.[19] Outsider, independent boards were more likely to have their corporations diversify. Insider boards composed mainly of managers were less likely to have their corporations diversify. Thus, the idea that independent boards restrain corporate diversification is false.

The Independent Board and Technological Innovation

The competitiveness of many corporations is founded on technological innovation that improves or supports their products and processes. These innovations are based on investments in research and development. Yet critics have said that modern corporate managers continually underspend on R&D. They assert that managers are risk averse, and that this risk aversion extends beyond diversification to R&D expenditures. The critics contend that professional managers wish to avoid the embarrassing failures that result from the inherent uncertainty of R&D. Therefore, managers will limit R&D expenditures in order to minimize their risk exposure. Once again, a board of directors composed of outsiders who are independent of management is seen as essential to reverse managerial risk avoidance and boost R&D spending.

The same two previously cited studies also investigated the effects of boards on R&D expenditure.[20] Both studies expected to find that independent boards led to higher R&D expenditures and both found the opposite. Boards with a majority of outsiders had lower R&D expenditures than corporations whose boards were composed of a majority of managers. It is the managerially oriented board that promotes R&D. The outsider board, far from promoting R&D, retards it. Again, a false trail.

The Independent Board and Illegality

Concerns grew in the 1970s and 1980s that a number of leading corporations were committing illegal acts. Managers were blamed and powerful boards of independent directors seemed to be needed to restrain the illegality. However, research has failed to support the idea that a larger number of independent directors leads to fewer illegal acts by the corporation.[21] One study finds quite the opposite—the more outsiders, the more illegal acts.[22]

It is presently fashionable to argue that outside directors should push managers hard to deliver performance and should replace managers who fail to perform. A manager under the control of such a rapacious board of powerful independent directors, in a situation where it is difficult to increase profits legally, would be sorely tempted to break the law in order to generate profits and appease the board. For example, a manager might bribe an overseas government to ensure a lucrative contract, even though bribery was against the law of the home country. Illegality is not necessarily bad for profits. In these ways, an independent board controlling managerial behavior could increase corporate illegality. Thus, the idea that an independent board will reduce corporate illegality is far from true.

The legality of board behavior may itself be questioned. One of the most serious accusations that can be made against a board is that it failed to look after shareholder interests. A board that is independent of management should take its fiduciary responsibilities more seriously and so avoid such accusations. Indeed, research finds that managers serving as directors and chair are more likely to be sued for failing in their fiduciary responsibilities.[23] However, the research also shows that they are *not* more likely to be found guilty. Hence, managers on the board raise suspicions, but when closely examined by the courts, they are found to be no more negligent or dishonest than outsiders.

The whole idea that managers will best serve shareholders when under the firm control of a watchdog board is suspect. Psychological studies show that effective senior managers are principally motivated by the need to have power and use it responsibly. The overwhelming majority of top managers like to do well for their companies. When top managers are being continuously checked by a powerful board of outsiders, they become frustrated. Their motivation is blunted and performance is liable to suffer.

Similarly, management writers have long stressed the benefits of unity of command, which makes it clear to subordinate managers who is the boss and whose directives they should heed. But a strong board of outsiders under an outside chairperson may create *disunity* of command. Decisions by the CEO may be vetoed or queried. Contrary orders may emanate from the board. Board decisions may lack internal consistency. Transparent board politics take managers' eyes off the real game of serving customers and beating competitors. Directive directors may sow doubt about the authority of senior managers in the minds of middle managers. Worse, if the board becomes central to decision making, the other managers may compete with each other and with the CEO for backing from the board. Such structural problems are liable to undermine the effectiveness of company management. At the extreme, the disempowered, compromised manager may become so frustrated as to lapse into passivity or leave the company.

International comparisons also do not support the idea that overall economic performance is lifted when an independent board acts as a watchdog and controls management. Japan has emerged as an international rival to the West. Its corporations have been a conspicuous success and Japan enjoys a large trade surplus with the Western world. Yet the number of inside directors on the board of the average Japanese corporation is 10.9. This is considerably more than the average of 3.9 inside directors on the boards of U.S. corporations.[24] Thus, Japanese corporations have more than twice as many inside directors on their boards as U.S. corporations. We note that Japanese boards are larger, and also have many outside directors. However, many of these are retired executives of the company. There is no clear evidence that Japanese corporate success has been based on the presence of strong, independent boards of directors that curb the waywardness of corporate managers.

BOARDS AND PAY

Boards are also said to have failed with respect to executive pay. Executive pay is big news, paralleling stories about the pay of entertainers and sports figures. Yet the discussion on pay is at best confused, and at worst destructive of incentive. When top managers were paid a straight salary, it was criticized for not aligning their interests with those of the owners. Thus, compensation based on corporate profits and stock prices was brought in, so that some part of managerial pay was risk and performance related. The aim was to reassure owners that any conflict of interest between them and the managers had been eliminated. When a company prospers, managers are well rewarded, thus providing incentive. The large payouts to top managers occur when company performance has been very good in terms of profit or share price rises.

Yet, when managers have received substantial pay boosts in line with performance-based plans, it has been roundly condemned. Great disparity between managerial and shop floor pay is said to incite envy and poor labor relations. Multimillion dollar payments to top managers are attacked as giving away the shareholders' money. But these very payouts are the direct result of the schemes installed to motivate managers and encourage them to identify with shareholders' interests. Such is the hysteria against managers that they are damned if they lack performance-related pay and damned if they get it.

There is evidence, however, that such financial incentive schemes do deliver more profits and so are working as intended.[25] Among large American corporations, performance-based compensation is used more often where the CEO is the chairperson. Mindful of possible criticism about having too much power and confident of his or her ability to raise corporate performance, the CEO seeks to reassure shareholders by having the board adopt a financial incentive compensation plan. Profits tend to materialize and so both the CEO and the shareholders benefit.

Nevertheless, the administration of such plans has been castigated, most vocally by the consultant Graef Crystal in his book *In Search of Excess*.[26] Crystal is incensed that, in some cases of below-par performance, the plans are amended to lower the level that produces rewards. This reduces the risk that the manager faces, so the manager supposedly bears less risk than the shareholder. However, the logic is false. The manager already bears more risk than the shareholder. Shareholders are able to hold a portfolio of shares across companies, so their risk is reduced and their exposure diluted. In contrast, managers are employed by only one company, to which their salary and incentive pay are tied. Moreover, their time and energy are invested in that company, making their human capital specific to it. Thus, the manager inherently bears a much higher risk than any outside shareholder. This is well understood among financial economists. Amended plans that make the share-based compensation of the manager less difficult to attain just reduce the higher risk the manager already faces relative to the outside shareholder.

Performance-related pay for executives provides an effective means of aligning their interests with those of outside shareholders. It is a very direct way to ensure that managers will act for the benefit of the outside shareholders. Modern executive remuneration practices should be seen as effective, rather than as evidence of the need for control of managers by boards.

CONCLUSIONS

We conclude that restoring corporate vitality via independent boards is a false trail. The trail is premised on the idea that professional managers of large corporations typically work against the interests of outside shareholders. However, they do not. Manager control does not automatically inflate managerial salaries or depress corporate profits. Modern managers who lack ownership may nevertheless work for the interests of owners out of a professional desire to use their power responsibly. Career advancement and higher pay contingent upon better performance also provide inducements. Thus, there are no real benefits in imposing greater control through boards of directors independent of management. Indeed, independent boards lead to underinvestment in R&D, which, in turn, retards corporate success. Similarly, independent boards fail to prevent corporate diversification and corporate illegality. The courts do not find that independent boards are superior in the discharge of their fiduciary responsibilities. Our examination shows that each of the arguments for independent boards is false. There is no basis for the present calls for reforms that would make boards more independent of management. Managers should be empowered to take action, rather than being shackled by boards of amateur outsiders who tell them what to do.

Despite our rejection of the call for board and chair independence, we recognize that board performance can be significantly improved. Many boards have a quite muddled notion of their role and how they add value. At one extreme, they act as society's police, emphasizing conformance and compliance, obtaining second opinions on every idea management puts up, and keeping management in check by delegating only minor decisions. These boards may well limit corporate risk, but at the same time shareholders rarely see much in the way of returns.

At the other extreme are the present-day media cameos of the board completely under the influence of management, more concerned with its status, perquisites, and rituals than with the fundamentals of good business. The challenge for boards, however, is not to seek needed improvement through simplistic structural fads such as "a majority of outsiders." Instead, board roles should be clarified, composition and membership should reflect competence and potential contribution, not old allegiances, and processes should be crafted to balance the dual role of boards in encouraging both managerial conformance and performance. The plaintive call for more nonexecutives will not solve all our problems. Figure 6.1 shows the position we are taking with regard to the need to redefine some key areas of board responsibility.

Our view of the essence of good governance was summarized brilliantly in a question put to the chairman of Exxon at a shareholders' meeting some years ago. The shareholder, a former Exxon employee, began by applauding the strong current performance of the company. "However," he continued, "I note that many of the positive results shareholders are benefiting from today stem from decisions taken by the past chairman and board members six or seven years ago, such as investments in new capacity and moves offshore. Mr. Chairman," the questioner concluded, "would you please tell us what you and your colleagues are doing today that will bear similar fruit in six or seven years' time?" A board that is unable to provide a first-rate answer to this question has failed the test of good governance, irrespective of its "independence" or adherence to immaculate processes for auditing managerial probity.

FIGURE 6.1

SOME ROLES OF BOARDS OF DIRECTORS

Traditional Roles	Proposed, Redefined Roles	Reasons to Redefine Roles
Develop strategy.	Review and approve management's proposed strategy.	The board of a large public corporation is an inappropriate body for developing strategy. Moreover, management should "own" and be committed to a strategy, and this is unlikely if strategy is handed down from the board. The board's focus should be on goals and performance, and on critiquing the credibility of strategy.
Set corporate culture.	Approve and foster corporate culture.	Responsibility for setting culture belongs to the management team, though the board needs to know and approve the ethical standards of the company.
Determine corporate policy.	Establish that policies on key issues, including exposure to various risks, are in place and are appropriate: review compliance.	Just as a board cannot initiate and determine strategy, it cannot develop policy in any detail. But it can insist that policies be developed by management, and that it be satisfied with the policies. It can also review compliance, but will have to exercise judgment as to how far this review ought to go.
Ensure statutory and regulatory compliance.	Require and monitor regulatory compliance.	The traditional responsibility description asks for the impossible. A board can be effective in setting standards with respect to regulatory compliance and monitoring. It cannot guarantee that laws are not broken, and the expectation of such a guarantee by many in the community is leading to unproductive "checking and covering bases"–type activity, and distracting from the performance focus.

Source: Frederick G. Hilmer, "Functions of the board: A performance-based view," *Corporate Governance: An International Review*, vol. 2, no. 3 (July 1994), pp. 170–179.

7

THE FUTURE OF MANAGEMENT

One theme common to all the false trails is that managers don't contribute much to the business world. The conventional wisdom is that management has failed and is beyond redemption. Consequently, corporations would be better off with fewer managers, since management really boils down to following hunches, getting out of the way of people doing the real production and sales tasks, or implementing someone else's canned approach. Moreover, managers must be closely monitored by outside board members. We, of course, have a much more positive view of the work that managers do and the contribution they make to their corporations. If redemption is the issue, management will be redeemed by improving on its traditional role, not obliterating it. Hence, we contend that the core ideas of hierarchy, structure, and analysis that have developed over decades ought be further developed and adapted rather than abandoned or radically transformed.

In fact, unlike most business prognosticators, who see managers as a species on the brink of extinction, we foresee a steady increase in both the number and importance of managers.

When other commentators on management see organizations growing larger and becoming more bureaucratic, with more hierarchy, managers, rules, and paperwork, they recoil in horror, making dire predictions that such organizations will sink under the dead weight of managerial ranks and red tape. The large corporation is then pronounced to be obsolete. In Darwinian fashion, it is to be replaced by swarms of new, innovative, smaller firms that have minimal formal structure, are light on their feet, and win through flexibility. These small firms require little management and so have few managers apart from their owners. The only alternative for large organizations, according to the pundits, is radical transformation— become flatter, leaner, big and small at the same time, intuitive, action-oriented, and clan-like. The elephant must learn to dance by losing weight, becoming double-jointed, and otherwise transforming itself.

The future, as depicted in this scenario, is a universe of bureaucratic megaliths and fleet-footed firms bereft of professional managers. It is a scenario of extremes. However, it is wrong on almost all counts. Maybe elephants shouldn't dance. If you want dance, find a dancer, but if you need logs hauled in hilly rain forests, elephants do the job quite well.

In contrast, we see managers as necessary and desirable, both in the large firms that will continue to flourish and in smaller and medium-sized enterprises. This is true for established industries as well as for newer, high-tech, high-touch firms. Managerial work will not become easier, though we recognize evolving differences as work forces, technologies, and competitive and regulatory environments change.

LARGE FIRMS WILL PERSIST

Large organizations are unlikely to disappear. Their size offers economies of scale and scope accentuated by the trend to globalization. In a borderless world, corporations serve customers across nations, aided by better transportation and communication and by increasingly similar customer tastes. Today, global competition is leading to the emergence of a few major multi-national corporations within each worldwide industry just as domestic competition previously led to a few major corporations within each national industry. For example, in automobiles, the United Kingdom used to have numerous manufacturers: Austin, Morris, Rover, Triumph, and Wolseley. These once-independent firms merged to form British Leyland, which then became Rover and is now a subsidiary of BMW. Similar processes occurred in the United States, where many firms merged into the big three corporations of Chrysler, Ford, and GM. Now U.S. majors are merging with companies on other continents, such as GM with SAAB and Ford with Mazda. Where is this trend likely to lead? In the direction of a handful of large global multinationals, each of which operates worldwide.

The same picture emerges in an industry far from traditional U.S. manufacturing, Australian insurance. This is a service industry in a nation of small population. Computerization has been extensive and handles much routine processing. If the pundits are correct, we should see the new world of small firms swarming and thriving through intimate service to customers. In fact, the Australian insurance industry is dominated by several large firms, most notably AMP and National Mutual Life, that are quite large by world standards. Moreover, the big are getting bigger and linking globally. AMP bought Pearl Assurance in the United Kingdom, while AXA, the giant French insurer, has just acquired 50 percent of National Mutual Life. Why? Because advances in technology have not favored the small insurer but rather have entrenched substantial economies of scale. Costs per transaction decline with increasing volume and risk can be managed more effectively in the larger firm. Indeed, the magnitude of these economies is similar to those observed in traditional manufacturing industries in the United States.

Nor does the shift away from manufacturing toward service herald the end of scale and scope economies. The service industries, as they evolve, will come to feature a few major companies of large size; witness the fast-food industry, with McDonald's and

Burger King, or the media industry or retailing or even theme parks. Some commentators on management still contend that high-tech industries, such as computers, software, and biotechnology, require small, flexible firms and that here the large corporation has no place. Small firms play an invaluable role in start-ups and innovation. But size continues to confer advantages in many aspects of high-tech industry. Intel, Microsoft, Fujitsu, IBM, Toshiba, ACER, the multiple telephone companies, and global drug companies are all giants. And as some large firms shrink, others take their place. In short, while smaller firms will continue to be formed and some niche players will always prosper, large corporations will be the only ones with the strength and resources to compete successfully on a global basis.

Managers in Large Firms

If large organizations continue, what of managers, especially the professionals who own little or no stock in the corporation? While roles are changing and will continue to change, and while demands for performance are increasing, nothing we have seen suggests that the need for managers will disappear or even shrink significantly. There may be fewer support staff as a result of technology or the contracting out of services, but the essential management function of defining and coordinating the work of hundreds and thousands of people remains. And hierarchies continue to be the most effective structure for carrying out this function.

Take the case of the Gillette Company, a leader in razors and a range of other consumer products. As described by Rosabeth Moss Kanter in *World Class: Thriving Locally in the Global Economy*,[1] the success of Gillette rests heavily on standardization, allowing identical customer needs to be met with identical products, irrespective of geography. New products, such as the Sensor razor, are most often launched globally with similar advertising and promotions. Yet such coordinated and directed actions are only possible with a clear and smoothly functioning chain of command. Of Gillette's 31,000 employees, some 8,000 are classed as managers and professionals, hardly a number consistent with the demise of middle management. And these managers are in continual contact, either directly or indirectly, with corporate headquarters in Boston, or with key product or regional offices such as the Braun headquarters in Germany. The systems and procedures by which these managers work, whether in accounting, finance, or personnel, are standardized throughout the global structure.

The increase in the number of managers at large global firms such as Gillette, Citibank, Nestlé, and Sony, however, will be fairly modest and generally less than the increase in total employees. For example, a tenfold increase in employees will produce less than a tenfold increase in managers because of the economies inherent in pyramidal structures. Hence, the increase in managers in the largest global corporations will be moderate relative to the total size increase of those firms, rather than being in any sense pathological or excessive.

The new large global corporations will increase the world's managerial ranks but they will account for only part of the total number of managers in the world. Moreover, while some corporations are getting bigger, the overall trend in the average large corporation is for employee numbers to shrink somewhat. Some estimates put this decrease at about 1.5 percent per year. Thus, the continuing increase in the size of corporations that emerge as global majors may be accompanied by a decrease in size of other large corporations. This may itself be part of the globalization process. The emerging global majors may grow while their numerous competitors may falter and decline, with the result that many corporations that were majors in their national market may fail to become majors in the new global markets.

Small Firms Need Managers

There is, however, another trend that will fuel the demand for managers. Considerable economic and employment growth is occurring in medium and smaller-sized companies. What is the implication for managers? For companies large enough to have professional managers in their ranks—that is, companies with more than, say, 50 to 100 employees—the increase in employees will lead to an increase in managers.

In fact, the small company unable to capitalize on the management process is unlikely to grow and survive its owner/operator. Once a small firm reaches a certain size, the owner becomes torn between continuing to build the business—finding opportunities, obtaining finance, negotiating major contracts—and remaining intimately involved in day-to-day control of operations. The way to cope is to develop other people as managers and become less hands-on in a day-to-day sense and more able to move the company to the next stage of growth.

Moreover, smaller companies have proportionately more managers than larger companies.[2] Smaller companies lack the economies of administration enjoyed by larger ones. There are many more managers in 100 firms of 1,000 employees each than in one corporation of 100,000 employees. Thus, the growth in size of smaller and medium-sized firms at the expense of some large corporations will actually boost the number of managers in the economy. In at least some countries, the national census data support this contention—that total numbers of managers are actually rising despite the publicized gloom about larger corporations downsizing and flattening.[3]

Management Roles Will Continue

Thus, managers are not an endangered species. They are increasing in numbers and becoming even more pivotal to organizations and to the wealth of nations. As each organization grows larger, it becomes more complex and more difficult to administer, thus placing a premium on effective management. The trend toward increasing administrative complexity is not due only to increases in organizational size. Size is important, but there are other factors that drive toward increased bureaucracy and administrative complexity, namely, increasing regulation and pressure from interest groups that represent particular constituencies or social causes such as the environment. For example, attempts to guarantee more equitable treatment for women and minorities lead governments to impose equal employment opportunity policies that generate rules about hiring, promotion, and deployment in organizations. Similarly, organizations in the public sector, such as education, strive to be more democratic by centralizing decision-making authority in a top board comprising representatives of students, parents, and teachers. Thus, the extension of democratic rights increases bureaucracy and centralization. Managerial complexity goes hand in hand with democracy.

In summary, we do not see the end of large corporations. Nor do we see that the growth of small and medium-sized enterprises will mean fewer managers. If anything, the converse is true. Moreover, this picture remains the same whether the subject is a traditional industry such as automobiles or mining or a new firm such as Nike, Microsoft, or McDonald's. Hence, the issue is not whether managers will disappear because management will become easier. Instead, the issue is how to prepare management to deal with the future and how to support what we see as a necessary good rather than an unnecessary evil.

However, unless managers address the "less is more" opinion of management that permeates the five false trails, they risk excessive regulation, unreasonable short-term expectations from the media, investors, and outside directors, and a consequent lack of support for the risk taking and innovation that underpin real success. For example, regulation in many countries is adding to the costs of raising capital, employing people, building new facilities, and dealing with customers. Much of this regulation is based on the false idea that managers are incompetent or untrustworthy and don't care about their own reputations; for example, regulation assumes that managers will readily mislead investors in their search for funds, or deliberately deprive workers of safe and fair employment conditions. Yet the benefit to investors, employees, and consumers of much of this regulation is questionable. Scoundrels find ways to defy the laws, while honest managers and the owners of their firms bear the costs of often unnecessary compliance. High and unreal investor and press expectations fuel the "quarterly earnings syndrome," whereby long-term actions are undervalued and all eyes are on the last quarter.

Managers can change these antimanagement views, though not overnight. The way forward, outlined in the next section, is for management to embrace the positive aspects of established professions, building on the achievements of the past both in management and in other fields.

MANAGEMENT AS A PROFESSION

Managers will continue to be needed in the firm of the future, and the task of management is likely to become more complex and demanding. Managers will be forced to be increasingly effective. Management's best chance for rising to the challenge and answering its critics is to become a high-quality profession. We contend that good managers are more likely to emerge and gain respect if management is viewed as a profession that develops and applies an evolving body of knowledge, rather than as a talent that defies understanding. The essence of professional management is the skillful application of sound and proven ideas to the particular situations facing the manager—not dogma, jargon, or quick-fix fads.

Parallels to the advancement of professional management can, we believe, be found in the history—both positive and negative—of other professions such as engineering, medicine, law, and architecture. Drawing parallels is hard, however, because there is no universally agreed upon definition of what constitutes a "profession." People calling themselves professionals now include dentists, veterinarians, accountants, surveyors, and, more recently, pharmacists, physiotherapists, actuaries, and quantity surveyors. The term professional is also being applied outside these areas to sports (professional boxers), entertainment (professional dancers), and commerce (professional salespeople).

What distinguishes a respected profession? In our view, a respected profession is distinguished by certain core values:

- Professions tend to be based on lofty ideals such as providing needed skills that the client is generally unable to evaluate properly, at least in the short term. It is the commitment to providing a service of value, even when the client may not understand or appreciate what is being done or why, that motivates a professional, not self-interest or enrichment per se. Moreover, a professional so motivated will more likely provide a real and lasting benefit to the client or the society. Conversely, an individual motivated solely by short-term gain can quickly bring a profession into disrepute, as has been demonstrated by the occasional rogue lawyer, doctor, or manager.

- Membership in the profession requires mastery of an evolving body of knowledge that typically takes years to learn and to apply skillfully. The knowledge is frequently highly specialized, for example, environmental engineering or pediatrics.

- The body of knowledge is based on sound reasoning. However, the type of reasoning used can vary widely, from the science-based approaches of the health sciences and engineering to the conceptual and logical approaches of law. The reasoning can also include aesthetic and qualitative elements, as in architecture, where factors such as "good design" must be considered.

- Professionals tend to have highly specialized language that allows precise and efficient communication within the profession. The clarity of language underpins both clear thinking and decisive action.

- Practice is carried out in accordance with high ethical standards. Any flagrant breach of standards is usually severely punished, ultimately by expulsion from the profession.

Members of a profession thus tend to be highly skilled and able to balance loyalty to the ideals and learning of their calling with the demands of those who hire them. The blindly obedient "corporation man" could not be a professional. Nor could the person who refuses to question established dogma or who flits from one fad to another. Professions evolve and have continued to exist because societies value the impartial and expert application of skill and knowledge. When societies do not believe that the profession delivers impartial and expert knowledge in an ethical way, its legitimacy and status are quickly eroded. Recent concerns about the legal profession illustrate the point. Instead of standing for lofty ideals, some highly visible lawyers are seen to be more interested in personal enrichment. At the same time, knowledge and reasoning are being replaced by drama in the courtroom. Fuzzy language—lawyers' doublespeak—and a few well-publicized cases of ethical breaches complete the picture. As a result, the professionalism of lawyers is becoming less credible and they are subject to attack and calls for regulation.

How, then, does management rate in terms of the core values of professionalism set out above? We contend that at its current stage of development, management would fail the test of professionalism, despite the liberal use of the term "professional manager." In this section, we explain why and argue that professionalizing management holds more promise than fads, false trails, or other simplistic shortcuts.

Ideals

One of the earliest examples of professional ideals is the Hippocratic oath, which since 400 BC has provided the basis for the professional practice of medicine, removing it from the hands of witch doctors and priests. The oath states that the practice of medicine is for the benefit of the patient—to further and protect life—and may not be used for deadly, mischievous, or corrupt ends. This is unquestionably a lofty ideal. When doctors are perceived by the public as not pursuing this ideal, their professionalism and status are attacked. Similarly, it is not surprising that the practice of law is tarnished when lawyers are seen as putting their own interests ahead of the ideals of client service and justice. Professional architects and engineers provide another example of lofty ideals in seeking not only to build and create but to do so in aesthetically and environmentally appropriate ways. The test of a professional is a preparedness to say no, to refuse to apply skills where to do so is contrary to the ideal.

The ideals of management are at best embryonic. Ideals have not evolved readily, in part because of the close relationship between management and economics, whose god is self-interest. If the best economic outcome for society is invariably achieved when all pursue their own interests, as Adam Smith explained in *The Wealth of Nations*, the management's credo might be "greed is good"—hardly a lofty ideal.

However, thoughtful economists would call that an incorrect oversimplification of economic theory. Given that most economic exchanges occur via long-term relationships, for example, with colleagues, suppliers, and customers, self-interest requires those relationships to be founded on trust, with each party respecting each other's needs. Ethics, altruism, and economics are not mutually exclusive. Good managers talk of leaving their organizations and the world a little better than when they started. Contemporary writing talks of management's obligation to "add value" over the long term rather than simply trade or speculate in spot markets. Managers are entrusted with assets—plant, equipment, ideas, reputation, money—and people. The goal of their craft is to transform the assets over time through the collective efforts of the people for whom they are responsible. Managers' concern for the ideals of their profession will lead them to create safer and more ecologically sensitive organizations, ones that provide goods and services that meet the real needs of consumers at a fair price.

A lofty ideal such as adding value does not have to be expressed in arcane or semireligious tones. Some firms, such as those in pharmaceuticals, can describe their goals in terms such as contributing to human well-being. But usually the ideals come to life in more down-to-earth phrases. For example, a senior General Electric executive talked of GE's appeal to engineers who like to do "really big things," such as building power plants or jet engines. He could have said, "We aim to use technology and science in large-scale ventures that benefit society," but probably few would have listened or been inspired. A company like Nike, built by people who love and believe in the worth of running and exercise, is another example of how a lofty ideal—promoting a healthy life-style—is given expression in concrete ways that a large group of people can relate to. Effective professional managers understand the importance of broad ideals and give expression to those ideals in tangible ways throughout their working lives.

Ideals are sometimes controversial. For example, some argue that a commitment to protecting the jobs and benefits of workers is an appropriate ideal, while others contend that this is secondary to the ideal of maintaining a competitive enterprise that has a secure future and providing goods or services that are in demand. For instance, for many years, IBM espoused the ideal of quasipermanent employment—until the market forced a reappraisal. The way through these dilemmas is for managers to be open and honest about their ideals, and to let employees, customers, and communities know when they are changing and why. Fundamental professional ideals, however, such as improving value and advancing society's well-being, are unlikely to change.

Defining a lofty ideal is often easier for an enthusiast than for someone who is just doing a job. The idea that professional management is independent of the primary activities of the organization, and that a professional manager could just as easily manage a steel mill, a film company, or a university, is no longer seriously argued. When managers have an intrinsic interest in the firm's business—running at Nike or big technical projects at General Electric—they are likely to be personally and professionally committed to its mission.

A professional value creator would, at times, say no to what he or she thought was an improper command. This would be particularly true when a command was unethical—for example, to deliberately lie—or when it undermined values by contradicting the body of knowledge on which good management is based—for example, to milk a brand for short-term earnings. We must recognize that this body of knowledge is still fairly fluid—as discussed in the next section.

Body of Knowledge

The typical modern MBA curriculum outlines the body of knowledge on which good management is believed to be based. The knowledge falls into three groups: learning the core disciplines, applying a number of disciplines to problems, and acquiring skills. The core disciplines include data analysis— the dreaded math and stats—economics, organizational behavior, accounting, finance, marketing, law, and possibly political science. Applied subjects that build on the core include corporate strategy and policy, change management, new product development, information systems, technology management, human resource strategy, operations, international and comparative management, and marketing strategy. Key skill areas include communication—writing, presenting, listening, interviewing—negotiation, numeracy and technical literacy, and interpersonal and leadership skills.

This body of knowledge is not exclusively Western, though it is acquired in different ways in different parts of the world and in different industries. The West uses formal education, increasingly, MBA programs and corporate and on-campus executive courses. A similar body of knowledge is used in the in-house management development programs of Japanese and European firms. Nor has this body of knowledge or ideas stayed static. The core disciplines have remained fairly constant. However, the applied subjects are growing and changing. Fields such as change, strategy, and international management are quite new. The emphasis on skills is also new. Previously, it was believed that the best way to learn communication, for example, was on the job, and largely via the sink-or-swim method. Today, most top management education programs cover both the ideas behind and the application of effective communication.

There are two types of issues with the body of knowledge on which the evolving profession of management is based. First, there appears to be an inadequate appreciation by some practicing managers of the knowledge that does exist. While managers are becoming more interested in learning, the interest is still quite limited. Second, the body of knowledge itself is at best embryonic, and at worst confusing and contradictory.

Limited learning. One of the newer themes in management is the "learning organization." The word learning, however, is used quite loosely. Learning organizations are supposed to learn from their employees, customers, and competitors. That is, learning equals listening and observing. But learning also means reading, keeping abreast of new research and new ideas, attending courses, and putting concepts to the test in practice. This type of learning is commonplace in more established professions, but has yet to become an integral part of being a professional manager.

The point came to life recently when one of us attended a major regional management conference, accompanied by an eminent scientist who was becoming involved in university management and wanted to attend one of the seminars. The keynote speaker was a professor of business administration who had written a book on international organizations some years before. The ideas he presented were taken straight from the book. The presentation was excellent. What amazed our scientific colleague, however, was the buzz in the audience that these ideas were "new." "Haven't these ideas been around for years?" he asked. "In science, if you were ignorant of something important that had been published years ago you would be considered negligent—don't these managers believe they have a professional obligation to keep up to date?" Apparently not.

Managers are not entirely at fault, however. Some academics have called for a "reformulation" of management ideas to make them user-friendly. Managers are seen as people with only a limited capacity to read about and learn from ideas. They are considered likely to be confused by the depth and complexity of theory— a common antimanagement belief. Thus, according to this school, ideas should be simplified, even if they are doubtful. All that matters is that the idea is appropriate and useful because it helps practitioners in some way.[4] As Andrzej Huczynski has noted, ". . . if engineers or doctors were taught such 'appropriate' theories they could kill either themselves or others."[5] For example, some academics have argued that managers should be taught that there are only a few types of effective organizations, such as simple structures or machine bureaucracies, even though research has shown that there are many, many different types that are effective, from small and slightly bureaucratic, to medium-small and mildly bureaucratic, to medium-sized and moderately bureaucratic, to medium-large and quite bureaucratic.[6]

Imperfect knowledge. A second problem is that the body of knowledge on which the professional practice might be based is far from perfect. Even the most robust management ideas are still relatively new and unproven. Hence, they are often hard to apply or turn out not to help in the process of adding value. For example, a key management task is to find new investments and make them productive. How are such investments to be evaluated? Finance theory provides a well-researched set of methods, using discounted cash flows adjusted for risks. However, in a world where uncertainty is increasing and new technologies and new ideas abound, projecting cash flows becomes almost impossible, and so new ideas based on option pricing emerge. At the same time, other noted researchers are questioning the whole idea behind discounted cash flows.

Such vigorous intellectual debate, however, is not of much help to practicing managers, and can even bring into disrepute the very body of knowledge that is being developed. Out in the field, the poor manager wants only to know whether or not to invest in a project. Yet we have observed meetings to decide whether to make a specific investment disrupted and distracted by fights between staffers, each pushing different methods of evaluating the investment, each supported by weighty research! No wonder practicing managers have become skeptical about the body of knowledge.

This second problem occurs because much knowledge of management is expressed in general terms that don't have meaning until applied. For example, if good management entails having a "vision," what exactly is this vision thing? Is vision a very broad statement like: "This company only does big things"? Or is it more specific: "This company only does big things in the electrical engineering industry"? Or is it even more specific: "This company only manufactures large electrical systems that sell for at least a million dollars and require large asset investments"? Another example of a general statement that looks meaningful until applied is "information sharing." When does information sharing allow information to be deliberately kept from managers—when a program of retrenchments is about to be launched, or a new competitive initiative is being planned, for example.

The third problem with the body of knowledge used by management is evident in the preceding chapters about the five false trails. Put bluntly, some of the so-called body of knowledge with respect to management is simply wrong. This sort of misinformation is supported neither by fact nor logic, and is thus no better than a guess. However, because knowledge doesn't come easily and because a knowledge base has flaws should not have us turn away from the ideal of developing a knowledge-based profession. Knowing what we don't know is invariably better than following false trails.

Sound Reasoning

All professional bodies of knowledge are founded on sound reasoning. The method of reasoning is not always the same, but typically it is of high integrity. Engineering, science, and medicine are based on the scientific method. Hippocrates, the founder of professional medicine, rejected superstition as the basis for cures and instead looked to reason supported by fact; for example, only use strong drugs after they have been tested and be cautious about prescribing remedies you cannot understand. Modern science follows the same approach—only apply those solutions that are supported by tests or real data because important things are at stake.

Lawyers use a different kind of reasoning, operating in the realms of precedent, principle, and logic. Their key is to seek consistency, to depart from established precedent and principle only when not doing so would lead to absurd results. Justice requires that similar cases be treated the same way until the law is changed by democratic process. Other professions use a type of reasoning that is more judgmental, taking account of factors like aesthetics. For example, the criteria for good design used by architects cannot always be reduced to numbers, but tests of form and function and concepts such as simplicity and symmetry help distinguish good from bad.

Management, however, is currently limited as a true profession because overall standards of reasoning are often low and there is little agreement on the types of reasoning that should be considered valid. That standards of reasoning are often low ought to be self-evident; otherwise, the dogma of the five false trails would not have so many supporters in both practice and theory. Moreover, at least partly because of the antimanagement bias implicit in the dogma, management has had trouble attracting intellectual talent from other fields. Even management academics tend not to be held in high regard as scholars within universities, including those with top business schools, although they may be valued for their ability to bring money and industry to the campus.

Where high standards of sound reasoning are emerging in management, there is often a bitter fight about the type of reasoning that ought be used to underpin theory and application.

On the one side of the ring are the high priests of scientific method who insist on large quantities of data analyzed via the most sophisticated techniques. For many, the analytic technique is more important than the findings of the research itself.

On the other side of the ring stand the case analysts. They advocate a more precedent-based type of reasoning: immersing oneself in the detail of a few cases and then extracting some general principles. However, to do this well and to generate findings that hold up over time is enormously difficult—recall what has happened to one of the best-known examples of this type of research, in the book *In Search of Excellence*. Ten years after this study, many of the so-called excellent companies had stumbled, and their fall from grace discredited some of the lessons drawn in the earlier work.

Although some leading business schools are recognizing the legitimacy of both kinds of reasoning, many business schools tend to favor one or the other type of reasoning. Some American business schools—Rochester and Yale, for example—have been torn apart by fights between the true believers of each approach. "If it isn't scientific, it isn't true," versus "if it isn't rich in behavioral insight and prescriptive advice, it isn't practical or realistic."

Finding a way through this dilemma will take a number of years. The good news is that both sides are actually using sound reasoning, with respectable antecedents. More progress would be made if they focused on the real enemy, the proponents of ideas that are unsupported by any kind of decent reasoning.

There is also cause for optimism in the position taken by leading practitioners with respect to basing decisions on sound reasoning. One of Jack Welch's precepts is "face reality." People who face reality, who dig out and respect facts, are the antithesis of the yes-men found in some of the traditional General Electric divisions.[7] Similarly, Harold Geneen at International Telephone and Telegraph Company insisted that decisions be based on "unshakeable facts."[8] Facts are the cornerstone of sound reasoning.

Our interest in a respected code of sound reasoning is neither altruistic nor theoretical. Professionals who respect and understand sound reasoning are also likely to apply their knowledge with greater care and skills, avoiding unwarranted guesses, shortcuts, and mistakes.

Clear Language

The fourth attribute of a profession concerns language. Professions typically use a number of words that define commonly used concepts and ideas. Outsiders often refer to these words as "jargon," seeing them as a kind of barrier that the profession erects to protect itself from competition or scrutiny. The language of lawyers is often criticized for just these reasons. Doctors go even further, writing prescriptions so illegibly that only pharmacists or other doctors—but never patients—can read them. Responses to the overuse of jargon include the development of products like "plain English insurance policies" and medical and legal dictionaries that laypeople can use to crack the professionals' code.

There is, however, a serious and useful side to the development and use of special language by professionals. What seems to outsiders like jargon is often an efficient means of communication, allowing complex ideas to be collapsed into a word or phrase. Words such as "irrelevant" or "hearsay" are in fact extremely meaningful to lawyers. Second, the jargon allows terms to be used in a precise way. When scientists say that something is "significant," they have a precise statistical idea of significance in mind, and this can be measured. By "feverish," doctors mean that the body temperature is above a specific number. Hence, the language supports the use of sound reasoning, for as Lord Kelvin put it: "When you can measure what you are speaking about, and express it in numbers, you know something about it; but when you cannot measure it, when you cannot express it in numbers, your knowledge is of a meager and unsatisfactory kind: it may be the beginning of knowledge, but you have scarcely, in your thoughts, advanced to the stage of *science*."[9]

How would management language be classified in terms of these criteria? There is no question that jargon is rife. "Strategists must focus on core and distinctive competencies to find holistic approaches for sustainable competitive advantage." "Human resource people counsel, consult, empower, coach, and inspire as they search for champions to liberate esprit via values and hoopla." Hopefully the people using this language know what they are talking about, because no one else usually does!

Such management jargon, however, fails in terms of being an efficient way to communicate precise ideas. Nor are the ideas well enough defined to help the reasoning process that underpins new knowledge. Figure 7.1 sets out a number of examples of the different definitions in business writing of the word "strategy."

We are indebted to Henry Mintzberg for four of the different meanings. Strategy is one of the most common terms in management-speak, but how does a person know which of the seven another person means? Even if there were only four possible meanings, there would still be only a 1 in 16 chance that both people meant the same thing at the same time! A CEO tells his division manager, "We need a new strategy for your division." The CEO wants a five-year plan that improves on current practice, with actions and resources clearly set out. The division manager comes back after two months with ideas on a

FIGURE 7.1
WHAT IS STRATEGY?

Author	Definition	Example
Mintzberg 1	A plan	Five year plan
Mintzberg 2	A pattern	Focus on high-value goods
Mintzberg 3	A position	Fast foods, not restaurants
Mintzberg 4	A perspective	Custom supplier, not mass producer
Ghemawat	Commitment	Major investment
Weick	Theory about past and current success	Exploiting an innovation
Henderson	Plan for developing and compounding competitive advantage	Aggressively building market share

Source: Mintzberg[10]; Ghemawat[11]; Weick[12]; Henderson[13].

new positioning or competitive initiative. The CEO sends the manager back to the drawing board or drops his initial idea. Poor language and poor expectations lead to poor outcomes.

Most of the false trails are built on poor language, loosely described terms that can mean whatever the user or listener wants. For example, what is a flat structure? How many or how few levels in a hierarchy define flatness? What is an action orientation? What is total quality management? What is a corporate clan or culture? How do we know whether one exists and whether it is the right sort to do what clans are supposed to do? Whenever one of these loosely defined ideas is attacked, its proponents simply redefine it. No wonder the dogma, even when potentially useful, is applied so poorly in practice.

Ethics

All established professions have and enforce ethical standards. Hippocrates spoke of the obligation to pass on and teach knowledge, and to exercise knowledge using the highest standards of care and skill. The oath also refers to the requirement to maintain patient confidences and to abstain from harming patients or abusing their trust. Similar ideas are found in the codes of ethics of other professions. There is also the duty to put the client's interests first, to avoid conflicts of interest, to be honorable and scrupulous in financial dealings, and to exercise high standards of care and diligence. When ethical standards are flouted, a professional body is expected to move in, holding hearings and taking disciplinary action that can lead to the loss of the right to practice.

Contrary to the negative stereotype of managers not caring about ethics, there are signs that managers are sensitive to a range of ethical considerations. A Conference Board study asked 300 international executives what they believed to be key ethical issues for their firms. These issues are listed in Figure 7.2, which also shows the percentage of managers who cited each one. Fourteen issues were seen to involve ethics by at least

FIGURE 7.2

IS THIS AN ETHICAL ISSUE FOR BUSINESS?

Top Issues	Percentage Answering Yes
Employee conflicts of interest	91
Inappropriate gifts to corporate personnel	91
Sexual harassment	91
Unauthorized payments	85
Affirmative action	84
Employee privacy	84
Environmental issues	82
Employee health screening	79
Conflicts between company's ethics and foreign business practices	77
Security of company records	76
Workplace safety	76
Advertising content	74
Corporate contributions	68
Shareholder interests	68

Source: Peter Madsen and Jay M. Shafritz, eds,. *Essentials of Business Ethics* (New York: Penguin, 1990), pp. 21-22.

two-thirds of the managers surveyed. They include employee issues such as health, safety, affirmative action, and sexual harassment. They also include the environment and community responsibility for advertising. In particular, there is a widespread appreciation of the problem of conflicts of interest, as in the acceptance of gifts. Thus, managers are perhaps more conscious of ethics than they are sometimes given credit for. The management profession is making some progress toward being ethically conscious. What is lacking is any mechanism whereby managers can police themselves through professional bodies that investigate and punish managers found to be acting unethically, in the manner of the disciplinary bodies of more established professions.

Many companies are now developing their own codes of ethics. However, most tend to reinforce and repeat obligations already in the law, while only a few set out broad value statements with respect to standards of integrity, care, or quality.[14] Moreover, the relationship between the ethical issues and the ethical guidelines is often weak. For example, a survey of marketing managers found that their perception of the extent of ethical problems in their firms was unaffected by whether their corporation or industry had a code of conduct.[15]

One of the more promising developments is that many managers are now recognizing that increased respect for people is both ethical and good practice. Respect for the individual is integral to ethical behavior. And it also improves performance. For example, the practice of treating frontline employees with courtesy, asking their views, listening to their ideas, and keeping them in the picture has transformed once adversarial labor relations. Similarly, being polite to customers—seeking to understand and respond to their concerns—is improving sales and marketing far more than another bag of money spent on advertising campaigns.

It is tough, for example, to maintain the balance required by ethical standards to respect people, yet downsize when needs dictate.

We do not pretend to offer yet another platitudinous or simplistic answer to what are real and pressing issues. But we are sure that until ethical codes for management are better developed, the professional approach we advocate will be hindered. Ethics underpin the skillful and careful application of ideas—a very different approach from the false trails, for it is generally unethical in professions to accept ideas without question and to apply them in a shoddy way.

ROLE OF MANAGEMENT EDUCATION

As teachers of and writers on management, we are concerned with the role that education can play in developing the professional manager of the future. Education is only one part of a person's development, though an important one, as we were reminded during a recent discussion with a group of chief executives. The topic was what future CEOs should be doing during their early 20s to prepare themselves. The first part of the answer was that they should get a good education through a sound undergraduate program. In the view of the CEOs, any solid program that offered intellectual discipline would do. Aspiring CEOs should also be learning leadership in team activities, both sports and social. Travel, for example, or backpacking around some part of the world, would provide an advantage. Such education and experiences were perceived as helping to develop the ability to cope calmly and logically with many complex issues involving both ideas and people, without fear of moving outside one's "comfort zone."

Once these aspiring CEOs begin their management careers, the next phase in their formal education is either an MBA program or short management courses. In our view, teaching on each of the tenets of a profession could be improved in both of these.

The lofty ideals of professional management are rarely discussed in management education, and if covered tend to be quickly dismissed with the words "It's a value judgment" or "Interesting question but let's get back to the numbers." We would encourage that more attention be paid to the goals of management and to its constructive and detrimental impact on society. These questions can be woven into courses that deal with more practical problems, such as introducing a new product, evaluating investments, or managing people. Asking who benefits, who bears the costs, and why the decision or activity, on balance, is worthwhile forces students to think about the ideals driving the business. These questions also develop a sensitivity to issues that are increasingly arising about the role of business in the community. Managers who ignore these issues do so at their peril, and should not be amazed when confronted with attacks from those who see no value in what the business is trying to do, or see the business as furthering its goals in unacceptable ways. Recent examples include the debate on censorship, which affects many media companies, and the debate on the environment, which affects almost all manufacturing and resource-based businesses.

Current bodies of knowledge are presented reasonably well in the better MBA programs. However, the contribution of

management schools to the knowledge base will be strength-
ened as they conduct more and better research. In our view,
this should be research on management, not research in such
underlying disciplines as psychology, sociology, or economics.
The knowledge most critical to managers is the causes of organizational effectiveness, with special attention to those levers
that the manager can pull. The focus should be on managerial
decisions that produce desired organizational outcomes, including more ethical and socially responsible ones. Many researchers in base academic disciplines overlook or disdain
questions of organizational outcomes, for their focus is else-
where, such as on the economy as a whole. Others fail to value
managerial effectiveness, seeing this as less important than job
satisfaction or the like. Thus, it is essential that management
researchers pursue a management- and outcome-driven research agenda.

Sound reasoning—both scientific and case method—is critical but underemphasized in education. Academics generally like
to teach their own discipline—marketing, operations, accounting, human resource management. There are only a small number prepared to teach the general processes of reasoning and argument, and even fewer who can do this in a practical way.
Finding ways to teach reasoning to future managers so that they
are better able to find and use facts, to see through false trails,
and to grapple with the variety of unstructured problems they
face is a major challenge for management education.

Clear language matters. In the course of writing this chapter
we examined a number of so-called management dictionaries.
They only highlighted what we pointed out—that the misuse
and confusion of language has become a real problem. Again,
educators and researchers can help by drawing students' attention to fuzzy language and showing how this can cause
problems. Moreover, writers can lead by example, pausing
from time to time to define their terms rather than gushing on
about globalization, participation, and strategic alliances when
these words mean quite different things to different readers.

We recognize that language and definitions evolve over time. The perfect and definitive dictionary of management terms can never be written. But without a respect for language, clear definition, and the importance of the use of words, it is unlikely that truly professional management will develop.

Ethical issues are dealt with in business schools, either in separate courses or as part of regular units on, say, marketing or finance. But ethics is still the "soft option," for in management there are few sanctions for unethical behavior. We have no ready answer to this dilemma except to say that educators should struggle with making ethics tangible or relevant. There will be failures and disappointments in this endeavor. But unless the effort to develop ethics is made, management as a profession will continue to be contaminated by the actions of the disreputable.

ADVANCING THE CASE FOR MANAGEMENT

The more professional approach outlined above will, over time, continuously improve management performance. And as performance improves, so will public perception and the policy environment. However, public perception is now quite negative, as evidenced by the popularity of management bashing in the media and by the vast increase in proposals for more regulation and even personally intrusive disclosure. Consequently, we believe that there is a need now to begin to improve the public's understanding, to redeem the idea of management as a valuable contributor to society. This is a job that can be done by management schools' improving their curricula, as described above, and by managers and their representative associations' becoming more effective public advocates.

Managers are not natural public advocates. CEOs who appear confident and knowledgeable in business settings often wither when confronted with a television camera or questions from reporters with agendas of their own. Nor are organizations whose function might be expected to be correcting misinformation about management, such as the Conference Board, the various associations of management, and business councils, much more effective. These organizations often see their main role to be political lobbying on economic issues such as the national budget or foreign trade. Improving the practice of and respect for management tends to be of secondary importance, even though it is talked about extensively.

Managers should network to combat unjustified criticism by external parties, such as the media, and should collaborate to resist unwarranted intervention by external parties, such as regulators or short-term investors. Managers should insist that their professional associations take an active part in advancing the cause of management. This includes running seminars countering the myth that all managers are corrupt, foolish, or lazy by illustrating the realities and complexities of managing, not the glib simplifications. Prompt public action should be taken when managers are found to have abused their positions, whether by incompetence or dishonesty, or the rotten-apple syndrome will continue to contaminate the barrel. Professional associations could also hold seminars pointing out why it is sensible to have managers who are not substantial owners running large corporations—that is, explaining the *raison d'être* of professional managers. Seminars on the pitfalls of basing executive compensation on performance in accounting earnings and also on share price would be salutary. There is a need to help people understand that outsider-dominated boards of directors can be counterproductive. The hazards of greater involvement in company management by investors, including activist investors and institutional investors, need to be made public. In short, there is much that can be done to broadcast the case for managers and to rebut the current clamor against them.

Ultimately, however, the onus is on managers to define their craft as a worthy one by their own actions and performance. When managers either agree with or remain silent in the face of the calls for radical change and complete abandonment of current practice, they implicitly add weight to the antimanagement dogma exemplified in the five false trails.

Management work is rarely simple or routine. The dilemmas of management include whom to believe and trust and for what, how to decide in the face of uncertainty, how to distill the signal from noise, how to impose order and direction on a messy situation to achieve a worthwhile goal. If management is so simple, why is sustained success so difficult to achieve? Why, in country after country and industry after industry, are fewer than one in ten firms able to consistently outperform their peers for even ten consecutive years? Why do so many firms move up and down the list of the top 100 or top 500 in their respective arenas? If there were simplistic shortcuts, instant success embodied in the five trails, wouldn't large numbers of people have woken up to this fact and reaped the benefits?

To us, the answers to these questions are quite clear. To achieve sustained success takes years of dedication, supported by the professional approach outlined above. Following this approach is quite different from jumping on the bandwagon of fads and false trails, as discussed in the next chapter.

8

MANAGEMENT REDEEMED

Having done our best to warn against fads and false trails, we now draw together our views about what professional managers should do. Our aim is to distill and summarize the positive ideas brought out by our analysis. It is not, however, to lay out our version of "the five principles of effective management." Even to attempt such a task would be at odds with all we have written about the essence of management. The discount tables in bookstores are littered with such books, most of which are useless. This book is the opposite, in part an antidote to books of that type. We are saying that you cannot reduce what effective managers do to a few simple principles.

Good management is too complex to be encapsulated in a canned program or universal prescription. Good managers need to have both a head and a heart. Their head tells them how to take some sound concepts and apply them carefully in each situation, using solid reasoning and collecting and respecting data. Their heart tells them that they have to take action in ways that bring along with them the people they work with and whose work they are responsible for. Every company, every group of people, and every market is different. Success cannot come prepackaged—it has to be worked at.

Remember, we are talking about large organizations—organizations of thousands, often tens of thousands of people, not the local shop or family firm. In large organizations, there are many operating units that need to be directed and coordinated. Managers do this work via the hierarchy. Yet this remoteness from the front line means that senior managerial work is abstract. Managers don't make the product, the manufacturing work force does that. They don't sell the product, the sales force does that. They don't make the detailed plans, the planning staff does that. Rather, senior managers review the work of subordinates, set strategies, establish priorities, authorize resource allocation, and so on. In doing so, they might be helped by the following lessons drawn from our earlier discussions on each of the five trails.

STRUCTURE

First, let's take organizational structure. Good managers don't treat organizational structure and hierarchy like some sort of dead, smelly cat, something to be kept out of sight and disposed of as soon as possible. They are not ashamed of having and using formal structures. On the contrary, they see structure and hierarchy as one of the most powerful tools available to guide the behavior of the people in their organization so that it performs well. For example, a manager wanting to tap into the ideas of people at the front line in order to fine-tune processes and improve productivity will create highly autonomous units, with lots of delegation and empowerment. This is a conscious choice, and it will be the right choice if the business situation demands incremental process improvement. But if the key to the business at a particular time is to provide integrated international service, the manager might choose an entirely different structure, whereby senior managers use their power and authority to put service standards in place and see that they are adhered to.

Often—McDonald's is a good example—both approaches will coexist. As circumstances change, so will the chosen structure and hierarchy. In short, we see structure as a dynamic tool, not as some idol to be fashionably flattened and destroyed.

Put another way, when managers ignore structure they get into trouble, as nearly happened to Nike. Nike is a modern, high-tech, high-touch company selling a range of running shoes and other life-style products around the world. When Nike was a small young firm, Phil Knight and his team concentrated on designing a product, getting it made, and getting it to market. The waffle-soled shoe was a great innovation and a wonderful success. However, Knight and his team had little time for financial controls, sales force organization, or planning. Structures were extremely informal. As the company grew, this style of management came increasingly under stress. How could production from a range of factories around the world be coordinated? How could selling campaigns based on expensive endorsements by sports stars like Michael Jordan be made to work without mechanisms to ensure an almost military precision? How could the massive flows of money be controlled without a strong and capable financial organization? The lack of a formal organizational process and hierarchy almost led to the undoing of Nike. It was only when the company began to take structure and process seriously that its future as a successful global corporation was assured.

ACTION

Our second concern is with the dogmatic belief that action in and of itself is a good thing and that reflection, analysis, and study are to be avoided. In our view, good managers welcome analysis. They are always seeking data and rigorously testing ideas against the data. They don't let themselves be stampeded by a false sense of urgency into "going with the flow." Good managers don't let the urgent drive out the important, but without a respect for data, reflection, analysis, study, ideas, and rigor, how

can managers distinguish between the urgent and the important? Making a fetish of action makes the "urgent crisis" seem
even more critical. The best managers are unafraid to say,
"Stop! Time out! Let's think this through before we jump."

We appreciate that speed is often the essence of competitive
success. And we are certainly not arguing against action. But
good managers aren't bullied into action by the macho notion
that thinking is wimpy. Moreover, they will worry about the
basis for their actions and be as certain as possible that their
actions are supported by sound reasons. This doesn't mean
good managers don't use gut feeling. They do, but they don't
make it their only managerial tool. They pay attention to data—
both hard and soft—and check out whether it's consistent with
what their organization is doing. They have a keen respect for
facts that challenge the conventional wisdom.

They can see, for example, how to gain a competitive advantage when they realize that a market that everyone assumes to
be homogeneous is actually made up of more than one distinct
customer segment. The sharp manager will then work out a
way to reach and serve each segment better by addressing the
customer priorities in that segment. Or they will notice that, despite the best efforts of their team, a product line or service is
running into fundamental customer resistance or competitive
challenges, and will withdraw before a crisis must be faced.

We are also saying that action isn't an end in itself. When a
good manager faces a tough problem—for example, sales are
slipping and the reasons aren't clear, or good people are leaving—what does she do? The Zen archers would say to concentrate hard on the goal and act intuitively. We, on the other
hand, would recommend that the manager think about and set
up a process for dealing with these problems. In fact, one of the
most powerful lessons managers tell us they take away from
some of our courses concerns the distinction between process
(how to attack a problem) and content (what a solution might
be). Zen archers don't care about process, they just want to
shoot arrows. Our good manager would structure a process

that would put the right people together and make sure they had the right data in front of them as they started to attack the problem. The nature and urgency of the problem would shape the process but there would be a process, not just an arrow flying through the air.

The folly of Zen archery is well illustrated in the following example we recently encountered. A large organization has been seeing its sales slip over the last twenty years. The decline has been extremely slow and masked by both economic growth and gradual increases in prices. However, like many similar situations, what is gradual can suddenly become acute and the management of this organization realizes they are fighting for survival. But they are good Zen archers. So two-hundred sales people were added in a bold and decisive stroke. Sales kept going down. Thus another arrow had to be fired. This time a range of new services was launched. The downward sales trend continued. No one took the time to analyze what was wrong with the core service. Certainly doing something might have been better than doing nothing. But doing the wrong thing—particularly in a big way—or not addressing the problem, was at best delaying the inevitable crisis and at worst hastening its arrival. Random action is not a universal good.

However, we do applaud executives who are prepared to act based on the knowledge, experience, reflection, and analysis that are central to their profession. Sometimes an unplanned action has unexpected results that turn out to be winners, like Post-it notes. But as Wallace Stegner wrote, "Accident . . . favours the prepared mind. Opportunity knocks only for those who are ready at the door."[1]

We are also for experiments. An experiment is a limited action done in a controlled way, and the results add to understanding. A major commitment is not an experiment, it is a bet. Our type of good manager encourages lots of experiments, but does so rigorously, without betting the firm or division, and with a clear idea of what is being tested and with a determination to measure and apply results.

TECHNIQUES

There is nothing wrong with good techniques. As knowledge develops, what was once arcane and difficult is reduced to techniques that allow far more people to do what previously could be done only by experts. For example, work study was once the exclusive domain of industrial engineers. Today, workers can be trained in how to analyze their work movements and eliminate unnecessary movements. However, it is a mistake to think that because employees have been trained in a technique they can just be left to get on with it. Guidance and support by managers, often including senior managers, are required for successful implementation.

Take reengineering, for example. Most reengineering exercises are dismal failures. Why? Mike Hammer and Jim Champy's book, *Reengineering the Corporation,* shows that when reengineering fails the underlying reason can invariably be traced to the failure of senior managers to understand or lead the reengineering effort.[2] Techniques alone are neither so simple nor so powerful that senior management's understanding and involvement are unnecessary.

We are not arguing that techniques don't provide useful frameworks or trigger provocative ideas. Good managers stay abreast of techniques but then apply them selectively and with great care and skill. Good managers are prepared to use their power and authority to adapt the technique and then ensure it is followed. They don't slavishly follow a canned approach, hoping it fits their firm.

The reason is that, in most cases, the essence of a firm's success is its uniqueness. Management, therefore, must be primarily concerned with creating and sustaining uniqueness, whether in brand, service, production approaches, people management, selling, or innovation. But uniqueness does not come from applying techniques as if they were cookbook recipes for good management. If this were true, the recipe would be quickly copied and uniqueness would be lost. Managers do apply generic techniques, as do architects in design-ing buildings or lawyers in drafting contracts. But it is the tai-loring and application of the technique, not the techniques themselves, that mark the true professional.

CLANS

A shared corporate culture can inspire people to provide high levels of customer service or to produce quality products. It's proven successful at McDonald's, Nike, Microsoft, SAS, McKin-sey, Toyota, Sony, and other companies. Meetings, symbols, equal-access parking lots and cafeterias, first names, informa-tion sharing, values statements, training sessions, retreats, cel-ebration are unquestionably a part of modern management.

Our concern is that the idea that the organization can oper-ate like a clan is wildly exaggerated. Nike, for example, always had a strong culture. It was founded by like-minded people who loved running and sports. They believed in the impor-tance of design and innovative products. They were also united by the fear of common enemies such as Addidas, Puma, and later Reebok. But they had to stop operating like a clan in order to survive. When Nike was in trouble, it was not the absence of clan culture that was the problem but rather the lack of finan-cial controls, sales disciplines, and integrated production processes backed up by a clear and accountable organizational structure. As these issues were addressed, Nike moved ahead. The story at Apple was exactly the same.

Corporate culture is like oil. Oil makes the car run more smoothly because the parts in the engine work together with less friction, but the oil is neither the engine nor the fuel. Nor is the oil the substitute for a driver who has to decide where and how fast to go.

Moreover, there is something very old fashioned about cul-ture. Today, most large organizations have to accommodate people from a range of backgrounds and cultures. In the com-petition for talent, the ability to do this can become a major advantage. Thus we see good managers creating an environment that is host to a diversity of approaches and cultures, rather than attempting to develop and promulgate a single dominant culture. Finally, we note that culture is not a substitute for the other things that good managers do, such as defining clear goals, rewarding specific types of performance, and allocating resources. These tasks, in our view, are closer to the essence of management than seeking to create some sort of clan.

BOARDS OF DIRECTORS

We don't believe that having tough nonexecutive directors looking over the shoulders of managers will resolve many of the problems that firms face. We are acutely interested in designing systems and structures that encourage managers to do their best in ethical and responsible ways. But in tackling this task we've looked at the facts, and the facts warn against the presumption that the outside, part-time director makes any difference to corporate performance or even to corporate criminality.

Good management is encouraged and sustained by good governance. But good governance requires much more than an independent part-time chairman of the board and a board composed of a majority of independent directors. We are concerned that this "remedy" will do nothing to deter unscrupulous managers from ripping off companies. Legislation won't wipe out greed and dishonesty. Moreover, this "remedy" may actually be quite harmful in terms of its impact on corporate performance. Managing a large public corporation is a demanding job. A CEO with a competent and supportive board is far more likely to cope successfully than one whose every action is under the microscope. A board that starts with the presumption of mistrust and incompetence is likely to find that it has created a self-fulfilling prophecy.

We would like to see a far more flexible set of rules with respect to board composition. At the same time, we recognize the need for enormous improvements in governance. Thus, we would argue for a performance-oriented definition of the board's role and for a greater emphasis on the competence of directors and their goal-setting and performance-monitoring roles. It is counterproductive for boards of directors to be turned into business police.

MANAGERS MISUNDERSTOOD

Corporate executives often seem to feel that they have to justify themselves to the public by explaining their job in concrete terms: "I'm not at my desk, I'm out talking to the workers and listening to the customers." "I personally taste the crackers produced each day." "I cut through all the reports and go see myself." "I refuse to read anything longer than a page." With the best of intentions, these executives are pandering to the audience. In doing so, they are making easy points but giving currency to misleading simplifications about the true nature of senior managerial work.

The leading managerial gurus of our time ceaselessly insist that management consists of simple activities such as walking around and talking to people, and they lend their prestige and credence to the image of the corporation as a kindergarten. Over time, managers may come to believe this description of managerial work and seek to practice what they've read or heard themselves preach. The abstract planning and reviewing of the big picture may be neglected in favor of concrete "show and tell" behavior that is really best left to more junior colleagues.

High-level management is about the big picture. It is separate from concrete practice, which is mostly delegated. A large corporation is made up of many pieces. The challenge of senior management is to make sure that each piece works effectively and supports the other pieces, that broken pieces are fixed and that new ones are created. The corporation's current activities must be related to where it wants to be in many years' time. Top-level management is about relations between objects, each of which may itself be quite abstract: customer service and brand positioning or the inventory and accounting systems. It is a game for chess and bridge players, as well as sports coaches, and it is up to individual managers and business schools and management associations to build a wider public appreciation of this point.

QUESTIONS FOR THE MANAGER

In conclusion, we cannot give you, the intelligent, thinking manager, a list of five easy lessons for effectiveness. That would be entirely contrary to the message and spirit of this book. However, our discussion of the five false trails yields some positive insights. Perhaps they'll give you the courage to abandon a trail that you suspect is false. On each of the five points (structure, action, techniques, clans, and boards of directors), we need to move away from fads toward an acknowledgment of the complexity of real management. The five issues should be seen as thought starters that invite careful reflection about your organization. They pose questions that you should consider. Think about these questions as applied to your organization:

1. Have you become preoccupied with downsizing, flattening, and informal work groups instead of aligning your structure and hierarchy with your goals?
   - When did you last use structure, hierarchy, and accountability to trigger and reinforce a major change or improvement?
   - Can you describe how each level in your organization adds value to the level below, and do the managers at each level understand their different tasks and accountabilities? Have you given your formal structure a fair chance to work for you?
2. Have you been cutting back on data, staff, and analysis to the point where you are beginning to feel uncomfortable about decisions you are making? Are you concerned that there are not sufficient solid reasons behind your actions? Are you sure your organization deeply understands its customers, markets, technologies, and economics?
   - Do people in your organization look down on those who say, "Time out" or "We really ought get more data"?
   - Can you distinguish experiments from commitments?

What was the last key experiment you conducted, and what did you learn?

3. Has your organization become increasingly attracted to techniques?
   - Are there a large number of techniques being used around your company and are these techniques often dropped after a year or so?
   - Are increasing numbers of managers going to short seminars offering quick fixes as opposed to more substantive and less prescriptive courses on management?
   - When your organization applies a technique, is a significant effort made to customize the technique so that the forms, questions, data requests, meetings, and decision processes fit into the way your organization works and make sense to your people?

4. Are "We need to strengthen or change our culture" and "It's all culture" becoming your main remedies to problems with service, quality, motivation, or communication?
   - Can you describe instances of how performance at the front line has been significantly changed because of some initiative with respect to culture?
   - How well does your organization deal with the diversity and potential diversity of its work force? Is the prevailing culture a help or hindrance in this regard?

5. Is the board mainly a watchdog and controller? Is it spending most of its time on conformance issues? Has it set believable overall performance goals for the company, and does it take achievement of these goals seriously?
   - Is the board's agenda dominated by conformance issues such as audit, legal matters, formal approval of decisions and reports, and compliance reviews?
   - Are directorships in your firm seen as sinecures, or is each director widely recognized as bringing first-rate competence and integrity to the deliberations of the board?
   - When did your board of directors last assess its own contribution to the performance of the organization?

The preceding questions are aimed at helping to clarify how the tools of management are applied in your organization. In addition, our arguments for professionalism raise questions about how the process of management is conducted and developed. Specifically:

- Can you articulate ideals about what you do as a manager? How does your work contribute to the common good? Do you feel that you are making this a more decent world? Would you be proud for your friends and kids to see what you really do?
- Are you building on and keeping abreast of the body of knowledge in management? Do you make time for serious reading updates and continuing education?
- Do you aspire to and insist on high standards of reasoning? Do you require arguments to be properly supported and facts to be well grounded?
- Do you use clear language in management and the management process in your company? Are words like participation, excellent, strategy, policy, and process used as gobbledygook or as ways to communicate precise ideas?
- Are you proud of your firm's ethical standards and confident that they will survive hard decisions?

These are challenging questions, their answers ought to provide some clues as to whether your organization is falling prey to fads and false trails, and how strongly it is committed to a professional approach. The answers may suggest what you might do differently. We believe that long-run corporate success is built upon investing in professional managers. Management will be redeemed by moving forward in the direction of the professions. It will, however, be undermined if it cannot shake off the preoccupation with fads and quick fixes.

NOTES

Introduction

1. B.H. Liddell Hart, *Strategy* (New York: Penguin Group, 1967), p. 5.
2. Eileen C. Shapiro, *Fad Surfing in the Boardroom: Reclaiming the Courage to Manage in the Age of Instant Answers* (New York: Addison-Wesley, 1995).

Chapter 1: Beyond Dogma

1. Michael Hammer and James Champy, *Reengineering the Corporation: A Manifesto for Business Revolution* (St. Leonard's, New South Wales, Australia: Allen & Unwin, 1994), p. 3.
2. Tom Peters, *The Tom Peters Seminar: Crazy Times Call for Crazy Organizations* (London: Macmillan, 1994), p. 3.
3. *The Oxford Dictionary of Quotations* (New York, Oxford University Press, 1992), p. 493.
4. Hammer and Champy, *Reengineering the Corporation*, p. 1.
5. Ricardo Semler, *Maverick: The Success Story Behind the World's Most Unusual Workplace* (New York: Warner Books, 1993).
6. Akio Morito, *Made in Japan* (London: Collins, 1987).
7. William C. Byham with Jeff Cox, *Zapp! The Lightning of Empowerment: How to Improve Quality, Productivity and Employee Satisfaction* (New York: Fawcett Columbine, 1988).
8. Adrian Cadbury, chairman, *Report of the Committee on the Financial Aspects of Corporate Governance* (London: The Committee and Gee, 1992).

9. Robert Townsend, *Up the Organization* (New York: Alfred A. Knopf, 1970).

10. Lee Iacocca with William Novak, *Iacocca: An Autobiography* (New York: Bantam Books, 1984).

11. Andrzej A. Huczynski, *Management Gurus: What Makes Them and How to Become One* (London and New York: Routledge, 1993), p. 277.

12. Noel M. Tichy and Stratford Sherman, *Control Your Destiny or Someone Else Will: Lessons in Mastering Change—from the Principles Jack Welch is Using to Revolutionize GE* (New York: Harper Collins, 1994).

13. "Why Warren Buffett's betting big on American Express," *Fortune*, 30 October 1995, pp. 90–102.

Chapter 2: Flatten the Structure

1. Frederick G. Hilmer, "Real jobs for real managers," *The McKinsey Quarterly*, Summer 1989, pp. 20–36.

2. Peter F. Drucker, "The coming of the new organization," *Harvard Business Review*, vol. 66, no. 1 (January-February 1988), pp. 45–53.

3. T.J. and Sandar Larkin, *Communicating Change: How to Win Employee Support for New Business Directions* (New York: McGraw-Hill, 1984).

4. David Olive, *Business Babble* (New York: John Wiley & Sons, Inc., 1991), p. 96.

5. C. Northcote Parkinson, *Parkinson's Law and Other Studies in Administration* (Boston: Houghton Mifflin, 1957).

6. Peter M. Blau, "Interdependence and hierarchy in organizations," *Social Science Research*, vol. 1 (1972), pp. 1–24.

7. Lex Donaldson, "For functionalism: the validity of Blau's theory", Chapter 5 in *For Positivist Organization Theory: Proving the Hard Core* (London: Sage, 1996).

8. James Brian Quinn, *Intelligent Enterprise: A Knowledge and Service-based Paradigm for Industry* (New York: Free Press, 1992), pp. 143–145.

9. John Child, "Parkinson's progress: Accounting for the number of specialists in organizations," *Administrative Science Quarterly*, vol. 18, no. 3 (1973), pp. 328–348; See Donaldson, "For functionalism: against politics and 'Parkinson's Law'," Chapter 4 in *For Positivist Organization Theory*.

10. Jan Carlzon, *Moments of Truth* (New York: Harper & Row, 1989).

11. Carlson, *Moments of Truth.*

12. Alfred D. Chandler, *The Visible Hand: The Managerial Revolution in American Business* (Cambridge, Mass.: Belknap Press, 1977).

13. Alfred D. Chandler, *Scale and Scope: The Dynamics of Industrial Capitalism* (Cambridge, Mass.: Belknap Press, 1990).

14. Ronald Dore, *British Factory Japanese Factory: The Origins of National Diversity in Industrial Relations* (Berkeley: University of California Press, 1973).

15. Koya Azumi and Charles J. McMillan, "Management strategy and organization structure: A Japanese comparative study," in David J. Hickson and Charles J. McMillan, eds., *Organization and Nation: The Aston Programme IV* (Farnborough, Hampshire, Eng.: Gower, 1981).

16. Elliott Jaques, *Requisite Organization: The CEO's Guide to Creative Structure and Leadership* (Arlington, Va.: Cason Hall, 1989).

17. Timothy J. Muris, David T. Scheffman, and Pablo T. Spiller, "Strategy and transaction costs: The organization of distribution in the carbonated soft drink industry," *Journal of Economics and Management Strategy,* vol. 1, no. 1 (1992), pp. 83–128.

18. J.B. Strasser and Laurie Becklund, *Swoosh: The Unauthorized Story of Nike and the Men Who Played There* (New York: Harper Business, 1993).

19. Robert H. Waterman, *Frontiers of Excellence* (Sydney, Australia: Allen & Unwin, 1994), pp. 35–46.

20. Ricardo Semler, *Maverick: The Success Story Behind the World's Most Unusual Workplace* (New York: Warner Books, 1993).

21. Wilfred Brown, *Exploration in Management* (Harmondsworth, Eng.: Penguin, 1965).

22. John Child, *Organization: A Guide to Problems and Practice* (London: Harper & Row, 1977), p. 62.

Chapter 3: Zen Archery

1. Karl E. Weick, "Substitutes for corporate strategy," in D.J. Teece, ed., *The Competitive Challenge: Strategies for Industrial Innovation and Renewal* (New York: Harper & Row, 1987), p. 232.

2. Herbert A. Simon, *Reason in Human Affairs* (Stanford, Calif.: Stanford University Press, 1983).

3. Robert G. Eccles and Nitin Nohria, *Beyond the Hype: Rediscovering the Essence of Management* (Boston: Harvard Business School Press, 1992).

4. Weick, "Substitutes for corporate strategy," p. 222.
5. Thomas J. Peters and Robert H. Waterman, *In Search of Excellence* (New York: Harper & Row, 1982).
6. Rosabeth Moss Kanter, *When Giants Learn to Dance: The Post-Entrepreneurial Revolution in Strategy, Management, and Careers* (New York: Simon & Schuster, 1989), p. 211.
7. Eric Schine, "Lockheed sticks to its guns," *International Business Week*, 26 April 1993, pp. 66–68.
8. Joseph B. White and Oscar Suris, "New pony," *Wall Street Journal*, 21 September 1993, p. A1.
9. Alfred D. Chandler, *Scale and Scope: The Dynamics of Industrial Capitalism* (Cambridge, Mass.: Belknap Pess, 1990).
10. Henry Mintzberg, *The Nature of Managerial Work* (New York: Harper & Row, 1973).
11. In Roy Rowan, *The Intuitive Manager,* (Hampshire, Eng.: Wildwood House, 1986), p. 19.
12. Barbara Block, "Intuition creeps out of the closet and into the boardroom," *Management Review,* May 1990, pp. 58–60.
13. Herbert A. Simon, *The Science of the Artificial* (Cambridge, Mass.: The M.I.T. Press, 1970), p. 44.
14. Jon R. Katzenbach and Douglas K. Smith, *The Wisdom of Teams: Creating the High-Performance Organization* (Boston: Harvard Business School Press, 1993), p. 39.
15. Philip W. Yetton and Preston C. Bottger, "Individual versus group problem solving: An empirical test of a best-member strategy," *Organizational Behaviour and Human Performance*, vol. 29, no. 3 (June 1982), pp. 307–321.
16. Weston H. Agor, ed., *Intuition in Organizations: Leading and Managing Productively* (Newbury Park, Calif.: Sage Publications, 1989), p. 13.
17. Weick, "Substitutes for corporate strategy," p. 227.
18. Elliott Jaques, *Requisite Organization: The CEO's Guide to Creative Structure and Leadership* (Arlington, Va.: Cason Hall, 1989), p. 9.
19. Michael Schulhof, "Why business needs scientists," *Scientific American,* November 1992, p. 96.
20. "Turn on a PC, tune in or drop out. But with a passion," *New York Times,* 28 January 1996.
21. Robert H. Hayes and William J. Abernathy, "Managing our way to economic decline," *Harvard Business Review,* vol. 58, no. 4 (July-August 1980), p. 74.

22. Neil Fligstein and Peter Brantley, "Bank Control, Owner Control, or Organizational Dynamics: Who Controls the Large Modern Corporation?" *American Journal of Sociology*, vol. 98, no. 2 (September 1992), pp. 280–307.

23. John Storey, "Do the Japanese make better managers?" *Personnel Management*, vol. 23, no. 8 (August 1991), pp. 24–28.

24. Miyo Umeshima and Ron Dalesio, "More like us," *Training & Development*, vol. 47, no. 3 (March 1993), pp. 27–31.

25. Alfred D. Chandler, "The enduring logic of industrial success," *Harvard Business Review*, vol. 90, no. 2 (March-April 1990), pp. 130–140.

26. "What do Japanese CEOs really make?" *International Business Week*, 26 April 1993, pp. 42–43.

27. Paul Milgrom and John Roberts, *Economics, Organization and Management* (Englewood Cliffs, N.J.: Prentice Hall, 1992), p. 426.

28. Graef S. Crystal, *In Search of Excess: The Overcompensation of American Executives* (New York: W.W. Norton, 1991), p. 205.

29. *Business Week* syndicated in "Rewards for US top brass hit stratosphere," *The Australian Financial Review*, 12 March 1996, p. 15.

30. Special Report on Executive Remuneration, *Wall Street Journal*, 17 April 1991, R-5; Milgrom and Roberts, *Economics, Organization and Management*, p. 427.

Chapter 4: Techniques for All

1. Ricardo Semler, *Maverick: The Success Story Behind the World's Most Unusual Workplace* (New York: Warner Books, 1993), pp. 65–66.

2. James Brian Quinn, *Strategies for Change: Logical Inceremental ism* (Homewood, Ill.: Richard D. Irwin, 1980).

3. Daniel Ichbiah, *The Making of Microsoft* (Rocklin, Calif.: Prima Publishing, 1993).

4. Tom Copeland, Tim Koller, and Jack Murrin, *Valuation: Measuring and Managing the Value of Companies* (New York: John Wiley & Sons, 1990), p. 24.

5. Copeland, Koller, and Murrin, *Valuation*, p. 132.

6. William G. Egelhoff, "Great strategy or great strategy implementation—two ways of competing in global markets," *Sloan Management Review*, Winter 1993, pp. 37–50.

7. Egelhoff, "Great strategy or great strategy implementation," p. 44.

8. Oren Harari, "Ten reasons why TQM doesn't work," *Management Review,* vol. 82, no. 1 (January 1993), pp. 33–38.

9. John J. Kendricks, "Companies continue to embrace quality programs—but has TQ generated more enthusiasm than results?" *Quality,* vol. 31, no. 5 (May 1992), p. 13.

10. Thomas C. Powell, "Total Quality Management as competitive advantage: A review and empirical study," *Strategic Management Journal,* vol. 16, no. 1 (1995), pp. 15–37.

11. Oren Harari, "The eleventh reason why TQM doesn't work," *Management Review,* vol. 82, no. 5 (May 1993), pp. 31–36; Richard L. Miller and Joseph P. Cangemi, "Why Total Quality Management fails: Perspective of top management," *Journal of Management Development,* vol. 12, no. 7 (1993), pp. 40–50.

12. Robert D. Buzzell and Bradley T. Gale, *The PIMS Principles* (New York: Free Press, 1987).

13. Kendricks, "Companies continue to embrace quality programs."

14. Michael Hammer and James Champy, *Reengineering the Corporation: A Manifesto for Business Revolution* (St. Leonard's, New South Wales, Australia: Allen & Unwin, 1994), p. 35.

15. Hammer and Champy, *Reengineering the Corporation,* p. 3.

16. Hammer and Champy, *Reengineering the Corporation,* p. 200.

17. James Champy, *Reengineering Management: The Mandate for New Leadership* (New York, Harper Business, 1995).

18. Schumpeter's ideas are described in Arnold Heertje, "Creative destruction," in John Eatwell, Murray Milgate, and Peter Newman, eds., *The New Palgrave: A Dictionary of Economics* (London: Macmillan, 1987), pp. 714–715.

19. Richard N. Foster, *Innovation: The Attacker's Advantage* (New York: Summit Books, 1986).

20. For further discussion see Frederick G. Hilmer, *Coming to Grips with Competitiveness and Productivity* (Canberra: Australian Government Publishing Service, 1990).

21. Frederick G. Hilmer, *New Games New Rules* (Australia: Collins/Angus and Robertson, 1989), Table 1, p. 77.

22. "USA: budgets for merit pay increases drop to lowest level in 20 years," *Business Wire,* 9 June 1994.

23. "USA: worker attitudes a larger concern than worker abilities, say a majority of U.S. employers, *PR Newswire,* 9 June 1994.

Chapter 5: The Corporate Clan

1. William G. Ouichi, *Theory Z: How American Business Can Meet the Japanese Challenge* (Reading, Mass.: Addison-Wesley, 1981).
2. Ouichi, *Theory Z*, p. 106.
3. Ronald Dore, *British Factory Japanese Factory: The Origins of National Diversity in Industrial Relations* (Berkeley: University of California Press, 1973).
4. Noel M. Tichy and Stratford Sherman, *Control Your Destiny or Someone Else Will: Lessons in Mastering Change—from the Principles Jack Welch is Using to Revolutionize GE* (New York: Harper Collins, 1994).
5. John Child, "Managerial and organizational factors associated with company performance. Part 2: A contingency analysis," *Journal of Management Studies*, vol. 12, no. 1 (1975), pp. 12–27.
6. John Child and Alfred Kieser, "Organizational and managerial roles in British and West German companies: An examination of the culture-free thesis," in Cornelius J. Lammers and David J. Hickson, eds., *Organisations Alike and Unlike: International and interinstitutional studies in the sociology of organizations.* (London: Routledge & Kegan Paul, 1979), pp 251–271.
7. Paul R. Lawrence and Jay W. Lorsch, *Organization and Environment: Managing Differentiation and Integration* (Boston: Harvard University Graduate School of Business Administration, Research Div., 1967).
8. Michael Lewis, *Liar's Poker* (New York: Norton, 1989).
9. Daniel R. Denison, "Bringing corporate culture to the bottom line," *Organizational Dynamics*, Autumn (1984), pp. 5–22, p. 18.
10. Joanne Martin, *Cultures in Organizations: Three Perspectives* (Oxford: Oxford University Press, 1992).
11. J. Rothschild-Witt, "The collective organization: An alternative to rational-bureaucratic models," *American Sociological Review*, vol. 44 (1979), pp. 509–527.
12. Ouichi, *Theory Z*, p. 91.
13. Ouichi, *Theory Z*, p. 92.
14. Tichy and Sherman, *Control Your Destiny or Someone Else Will*, p. 407.
15. Tichy and Sherman, *Control Your Destiny or Someone Else Will*, p. 107.
16. William Rodgers, *Think: A Biography of the Watsons and IBM* (New York: Signet, 1970), p. x.

Chapter 6: The Board of Directors as Watchdog

1. Robert A.G. Monks and Nell Minow, *Power and Accountability: Restoring the Balance of Power Between Corporations, Owners, and Society* (New York: Harper Business, 1991).
2. Adrian Cadbury, Chairman, *Report of the Committee on the Financial Aspects of Corporate Governance* (London: The Committee and Gee, 1992).
3. Idalene F. Kesner and Dan R. Dalton, "Boards of directors and the checks and (im)balances of corporate governance," *Business Horizons,* September-October 1986, pp. 17–23.
4. Kesner and Dalton, "Boards of directors and the checks and (im)balances of corporate governance."
5. Myles L. Mace, *Directors: Myth and Reality* (Boston: Harvard University Graduate School of Business Administration, Research Div., 1971).
6. Gideon Chitayat, "Working relationships between the chairman of the board of directors and the CEO," *Management International Review,* vol. 25 (1985), pp. 65–70.
7. Mace, *Directors.*
8. Monks and Minow, *Power and Accountability.*
9. Michael C. Jensen, "Eclipse of the public corporation," *Harvard Business Review,* September-October 1989, pp. 61–74.
10. Adolf A. Berle, Jr., and Gardiner C. Means, *The Modern Corporation and Private Property* (New York: Harcourt, Brace, & World, 1968).
11. George J. Stigler and Claire Friedland, "The literature of economics: The case of Berle and Means," *Journal of Law and Economics,* vol. 26 (1983), pp. 237–268.
12. John Kenneth Galbraith, *A Short History of Financial Euphoria* (New York: Whittle Direct Books, 1990), pp. 78–80.
13. Lex Donaldson and James H. Davis, "Boards and company performance—research challenges the conventional wisdom," *Corporate Governance,* vol. 2, no. 3 (July 1994), pp. 151–160.
14. Stanley C. Vance, *Boards of Directors: Structure and Performance* (Eugene: University of Oregon Press, 1964), p. 5.
15. Stanley C. Vance, "Corporate governance: Assessing corporate performance by boardroom attributes," *Journal of Business Research,* no. 6 (1978), pp. 203–220.
16. Donaldson and Davis, "Boards and company performance."
17. Lex Donaldson and James H. Davis, "Stewardship theory or agency theory: CEO governance and shareholder returns," *Australian Journal of Management,*" vol. 16 (July 1991), pp. 49–64.

18. Brian K. Boyd, "CEO duality and firm performance: A contingency model," *Strategic Management Journal,* 16 May 1995, pp. 301–312.
19. Barry D. Baysinger and Henry N. Butler, "Corporate governance and the board of directors: Performance effects of changes in board composition," *Journal of Law, Economics and Organization,* vol. 1, no. 1 (Spring 1985), pp. 101–124; Charles W.L. Hill and Scott A. Snell, "External control, corporate strategy, and firm performance in research-intensive industries," *Strategic Management Journal,* vol. 9 (1988), pp. 577–590.
20. Baysinger and Butler, "Corporate governance and the board of directors"; Hill and Snell, "External control, corporate strategy, and firm performance."
21. Kesner and Dalton, "Boards of directors and the checks and (im)balances of corporate governance."
22. Frederick H. Gautschi, III, and Thomas M. Jones, "Illegal corporate behavior and corporate board structure," *Research in Corporate Social Performance and Policy,* vol. 9 (1987), pp. 93–106.
23. Idalene F. Kesner and Roy B. Johnson, "An investigation of the relationship between board composition and stockholder suits," *Strategic Management Journal,* vol. 11, no. 41 (1990), pp. 327–336.
24. D.R. Dalton and I.F. Kesner, "Composition and CEO duality in boards of directors: An international perspective," *Journal of International Business,* vol. 18, no. 3 (1987), pp. 33–42.
25. James H. Davis and Lex Donaldson, "Executive Compensation, Corporate Governance and the Wealth of Corporations," Working Paper, Australian Graduate School of Management, Kensington, New South Wales (February 1996).
26. Graef S. Crystal, *In Search of Excess: The Overcompensation of American Executives* (New York: W.W. Norton, 1991), p. 205.

Chapter 7: The Future of Management

1. Rosabeth Moss Kanter, *World Class: Thriving Locally in the Global Economy* (New York: Simon & Schuster, 1995).
2. Peter M. Blau, "Interdependence and hierarchy in organizations," *Social Science Research* (1), pp. 1–24; Peter M. Blau and P.A. Schoenherr, *The Structure of Organizations* (New York: Basic Books, 1971); Lex Donaldson, *For Positivist Organization Theory: Proving the Hard Core* (London: Sage, 1996).

3. Craig R. Littler, Thomas Bramble, and Jacquie McDonald, *Organisational Restructuring: Downsizing, Delayering and Managing Change at Work* (Canberra, Australia: Department of Industrial Relations, 1994).
4. Andrzej A. Huczynski, *Management Gurus: What Makes Them and How to Become One* (London and New York: Routledge, 1993), p. 9.
5. Huczynski, *Management Gurus*, p. 10.
6. Danny Miller, "Configurations of strategy and structure: Towards a synthesis," *Strategic Management Journal*, 7 (1986), pp. 233–249; Henry Mintzberg, *The Structuring of Organizations: A Synthesis of Research* (Englewood Cliffs, N.J.: Prentice Hall, 1979). For a critique, see Donaldson, *For Positivist Organization Theory*, chapter 6.
7. Noel M. Tichy and Stratford Sherman, *Control Your Destiny or Someone Else Will* (New York: Harper Business, 1994), p. 112.
8. Harold S. Geneen with Alvin Moscow, *Managing* (London: Grafton Books, 1988), pp. 77–78.
9. William Thomson, Lord Kelvin "Popular lectures and addresses (1891–1894)" in John Bartlett, *Bartlett's Familiar Quotations* (Boston, Little Brown & Company, 1968).
10. Henry Mintzberg, *The Rise and Fall of Strategic Planning* (New York: Free Press, 1994), pp. 21–32.
11. Pankaj Ghemawat, *Commitment: The Dynamic of Strategy* (New York: Free Press, 1991).
12. Karl Weick, "Substitutes for strategy," in D.J. Teece, ed., *The Competitive Challenge: Strategies for Industrial Innovation and Renewal* (New York: Harper & Row, 1987), pp. 221–233.
13. Bruce D. Henderson, "The origin of strategy," *Harvard Business Review*, November-December 1989, pp. 139–143.
14. Peter Madsen and Jay M. Shafritz, eds., *Essentials of Business Ethics* (New York: Penguin, 1990), p. 224.
15. Madsen and Shafritz, *Essentials of Business Ethics*, p. 223.

Chapter 8: Conclusions

1. Wallace Stegner, *Recapitulation* (Lincoln: University of Nebraska Press, 1979), p. 165.
2. Michael Hammer and James Champy, *Reengineering the Corporation: A Manifesto for Business Revolution* (St. Leonard's, New South Wales, Australia: Allen & Unwin, 1994), p. 35.

INDEX

ACKNOWLEDGMENTS

We should like to extend our appreciation to the many people who helped us in the production of this book. To Orginia Charteris, a big thank you for tirelessly typing and retyping the manuscript as we endlessly rewrote and polished it. To Beth Anderson of The Free Press, for being such a good editor, quickly grasping the novel nature of our project and providing succinct edits of our prose. To June Ohlson, for assistance in research and copy editing to make the manuscript as accessible as possible to the reader. To Pamela Taylor and the willing staff of the Frank Lowy Library at the Australian Graduate School of Management, for their help in finding source materials. To Matthew Stubbs, for acting as research assistant. To our many colleagues at the AGSM and in industry whose input and encouragement were invaluable. To the countless managers whose experiences we have leaned on throughout the text. And, last but not least, to our families, without whose support the book would have been impossible and to whom we dedicate this book.